The World of Jesus

Series Description

Putting the Bible in Its Place is a series of books designed to provide modern Bible readers with an introduction to the backgrounds of the most prominent biblical characters. Just as Jesus was fully God and a fully human man of first-century Galilee, the biblical texts are both the eternal Word of God and ancient literature reflecting the events, customs, and conventions of their time. There are many resources that address the spiritual message of the Bible, but fewer that treat the ancient historical and cultural contexts in a way that is accessible to non-specialists. The volumes in this series will introduce Bible readers to the worlds of important figures like Abraham, Moses, David, Jezebel, Esther, Mary, and Paul. They will span the entire chronology of Israelite and early church history, from about 2000 B.C. to the end of the first century A.D.

Throughout this period, the world experienced dramatic changes. Empires rose from obscurity to world domination, only to crumble into the dust. People migrated from land to land—often, not by any choice of their own. New languages and literary styles took the places of the old. Technology advanced dramatically. Ancient customs were altered or abandoned. Old gods were exchanged for new. No single volume could adequately survey the histories and cultures of these diverse times and situations. Each volume in this series captures but a slice of the picture. But together, they will provide the reader with a comprehensive orientation to the world where the people of the Bible lived, worked, wrote, or ruled.

These volumes are designed for the general reader, not the scholar. We assume our readers will have little knowledge of the current state of academic biblical studies, and that they are more interested in the big picture than points of scholarly controversy. While we include many references to the Bible and to ancient sources, we generally omit references to modern secondary literature, except for some studies describing recent discoveries or major new perspectives. At the end of each volume there is a bibliography that includes sources that address many issues in greater detail and with more discussion of scholarly opinions. While all of these texts will be useful to those wishing to delve deeper into biblical studies, readers should be aware that they come from a variety of perspectives, and some may challenge the readers' theological views or preconceptions. Read them critically, comparing and contrasting the opinions expressed in different texts. Scholars, too, have their own biases and points of view, shaped by their historical (and personal) contexts.

Anthony J. Tomasino
Series Editor
Volumes in the Series:
1. Anthony J. Tomasino, The World of Jesus

The World of Jesus

Putting the Bible in Its Place

ANTHONY J. TOMASINO

SERIES EDITOR
ANTHONY J. TOMASINO

WIPF & STOCK · Eugene, Oregon

THE WORLD OF JESUS
Putting the Bible in Its Place

Copyright © 2011 Anthony J. Tomasino. All rights reserved. Except for brief quotations in critical publications or reviews, no part of this book may be reproduced in any manner without prior written permission from the publisher. Write: Permissions, Wipf and Stock Publishers, 199 W. 8th Ave., Suite 3, Eugene, OR 97401.

Wipf & Stock
An Imprint of Wipf and Stock Publishers
199 W. 8th Ave., Suite 3
Eugene, OR 97401
www.wipfandstock.com

ISBN 13: 978-1-60899-137-2

Manufactured in the U.S.A.

All scripture quotations, unless otherwise indicated, are the author's translation.

Contents

Timeline vii
Abbreviations ix

1. Jesus According to the Bible 1
2. Windows into the Past 9
3. The Land and Its Peoples 27
4. The Historical Context 35
5. The Government 69
6. The Cultural Context 83
7. Jesus' Religious Context 107
8. Jesus in His "Place" 136

Bibliography 149
Scripture Index 153
Subject Index 158

Timeline

YEAR	PERSON/EVENT	BIBLE BOOKS
ca. 2000 BC	ABRAHAM The Patriarchs in Canaan	GENESIS
1800 BC	Israel in Egypt	
1600 BC	Enslavement of Israelites	EXODUS
1400 BC	MOSES (?) and the Exodus	EXODUS, LEVITICUS, NUMBERS, DEUTERONOMY
	Joshua Era of the Judges	JOSHUA JUDGES
1200 BC		RUTH
	Saul, first king of Israel	1 SAMUEL
1000 BC	KING DAVID Solomon Israel divides into two kingdoms	1–2 SAMUEL, 1 CHRONICLES 1 KINGS, 2 CHRONICLES
	Ahab and JEZEBEL Rise of Assyria	2 KINGS, 2 CHRONICLES

Timeline

800 BC	ISAIAH Fall of Northern Kingdom (Israel)	AMOS, HOSEA, MICAH, ISAIAH 2 KINGS, 2 CHRONICLES
	King Josiah's Reforms Rise of Babylon	2 KINGS, 2 CHRONICLES, ISAIAH JEREMIAH
600 BC	Fall of Judah—Babylonian Exile, DANIEL Persian Empire conquers Babylon Completion of Second Temple	JEREMIAH, EZEKIEL 2 KINGS, 2 CHRONICLES DANIEL, HAGGAI, ZECHARIAH
	ESTHER EZRA and Nehemiah	ESTHER EZRA, NEHEMIA, MALACHI
400 BC	Alexander the Great conquers Persia Greeks rule over Judea	
200 BC	The Hasmonean Revolt and Dynasty	(The Apocrypha)
	Roman conquest of Judea MARY	
AD 1	JESUS Peter and James PAUL Death of JOHN	GOSPELS ACTS NEW TESTAMENT EPISTLES REVELATION
AD 100		

Abbreviations

Old Testament

Gen	Genesis
Exod	Exodus
Lev	Leviticus
Num	Numbers
Deut	Deuteronomy
Josh	Joshua
Judg	Judges
Ruth	Ruth
1–2 Sam	1–2 Samuel
1–2 Kgs	1–2 Kings
1–2 Chr	1–2 Chronicles
Ezra	Ezra
Neh	Nehemiah
Esth	Esther
Job	Job
Ps/Pss	Psalms
Prov	Proverbs
Eccl	Ecclesiastes
Song	Song of Songs
Isa	Isaiah
Jer	Jeremiah
Lam	Lamentations

Ezek	Ezekiel
Dan	Daniel
Hos	Hosea
Joel	Joel
Amos	Amos
Obad	Obadiah
Mic	Micah
Nah	Nahum
Hab	Habakkuk
Zeph	Zephaniah
Hag	Haggai
Zech	Zechariah
Mal	Malachi

New Testament

Matt	Matthew
Mark	Mark
Luke	Luke
John	John
Acts	Acts
Rom	Romans
1–2 Cor	1–2 Corinthians
Gal	Galatians
Eph	Ephesians
Phil	Philippians
Col	Colossians
1–2 Thess	1–2 Thessalonians
1–2 Tim	1–2 Timothy
Titus	Titus

Phlm	Philemon
Heb	Hebrews
Jas	James
1–2 Pet	1–2 Peter
1–2–3 John	1–2–3 John
Jude	Jude
Rev	Revelation

Apocrypha

1–2 Macc	1–2 Maccabees
Tob	Tobit
Sir	Ben Sira (Ecclesiasticus)
2 Bar	2 Baruch

Rabbinic Literature

m.	*Mishnah*
b.	*Babylonian Talmud*
y.	*Jerusalem Talmud (Talmud Yerushalmi)*
Abot	*Aboth*
B.Bat.	*Baba Batra*
B. Qam.	*Baba Qamma*
Git.	*Gittin*
Hul.	*Hullin*
Ketub.	*Ketubbot*
Meg.	*Megillah*
Mid.	*Middot*
Sanh.	*Sanhedrin*
Shabb.	*Shabbat*
Ta`an	*Ta`anit*

Josephus

Jos.	Josephus
Life	The Life of Flavius Josephus
Ag. Ap.	Against Apion
Ant.	Jewish Antiquities
War	Jewish War

1

Jesus According to the Bible

AT THE CROSSROADS OF history, we encounter the person of Jesus. Jesus was born in a time when the center of the world was tilting to the West. For millennia, the Near East, the very cradle of civilization, had been the focal point of world events. But now, the people who had given the world agriculture, animal husbandry, and writing had been surpassed by the beneficiaries of their brilliance. The great empires that had ruled the East—Assyria, Babylon, and Persia—were fading memories. The current overlords of Judea had not come marching across the deserts in clouds of dust. Rather, they had come sailing from afar, aboard swift vessels driven by the winds or powered by the sweat of slaves. Their languages were strange. Their customs were abhorrent. Their might was irresistible. The sun was setting on the East, and rising on the West.

JESUS' CHILDHOOD

The Gospel accounts place the birth of Jesus at the beginning of the Roman Empire. Judea had been conquered by Rome in 63 BC, a casualty of the cataclysmic clashes of generals that brought down the old Roman Republic and paved the way for the rise of a new political organization. Sometimes, the affairs of state were administered by Roman governors, foreigners charged with the tasks of collecting taxes and keeping the unruly barbarians in line. But at the time of Jesus' birth, Judea was under the capricious command of Herod the Great, a "client king" under Roman authority. Jesus' birth occurred in the final years of Herod's infamous reign.

THE WORLD OF JESUS

According to the first chapters of Matthew and Luke, Jesus was conceived miraculously, formed in the womb of the Virgin Mary by the power of God. At the time when she conceived, Mary was already betrothed to a man named Joseph, and the news of her pregnancy threatened to cause a scandal. But when Joseph was assured in a dream that the child had been conceived by the Holy Spirit, he agreed to take Mary as his wife (Matt 1:19–25). Mary and Joseph were residents of Nazareth, a town of Galilee (north of Judea). But when the Roman emperor required that everyone return to his ancestral home for inclusion in a census, Joseph traveled with his expectant wife to Bethlehem in Judea (Luke 2:1–3). It was there that Jesus was born, in fulfillment of Micah's prophecy (Mic 5:2) that the Messiah would come forth from Bethlehem. When King Herod learned that a child had been born who was being hailed as the king of the Jews, he sought to kill the baby Jesus. The Holy Family fled to Egypt, where they remained until after Herod had died. Jesus and his family then returned to their home in Galilee (Matt 2:1–15).

The Gospels say little about Jesus' boyhood. Luke tells us that when Jesus was a child, he amazed the teachers of the Law with his learning (Luke 2:41–52). But other than this incident, the canonical Gospels pass over Jesus' youth without comment, which can probably be taken as evidence that his boyhood was generally unremarkable. Most likely, Jesus was trained by Joseph to be a carpenter. His religious education would have occurred in his home and in the local synagogue.

JESUS' TEACHING

But when Jesus was about thirty years old (Luke 3:23), his life took an abrupt departure from the normal course of career and family. At this time, Jesus was attracted to the teachings of John the Baptist (who is identified in Luke 1 as Jesus' cousin). When John baptized Jesus, there was a miraculous manifestation of the Holy Spirit, and John testified that Jesus was the Messiah (Matt 3:13–17; Mark 1:9–11; Luke 3:21–22; John 1:29–36). Jesus then endured a forty day fast in the wilderness before he embarked on his own ministry (Matt 4:1–11; Mark 1:12–13; Luke 4:1–13). He gathered around himself a band of twelve disciples (students), and began to wander through Galilee, preaching the repentance of sin.

The Gospels do not present chronological accounts of Jesus' ministry. Rather, the way they order and organize their material is determined by their unique theological or rhetorical purposes. Nonetheless, there is general agreement in their accounts of Jesus' work. Jesus began his preaching ministry in Galilee, picking up the same theme that had occupied John the Baptist: the Kingdom of God (Matt 4:12–17; Mark 1:14–15).[1] The Kingdom of God was to be a radical transformation of the world order, initiated by God himself, which would eventually displace the kingdoms of this world. Jesus taught his disciples that the Kingdom would not be established with violence, because it was not like the kingdoms of earth (John 18:36). It would come into existence gradually, like the growth of a mustard plant or like yeast that slowly leavens a loaf of bread (Matt 13:31–35). Through parables, object lessons, and biblical exposition, Jesus explained to his listeners that the Kingdom of God was being initiated by his ministry, and would find its consummation when he was manifested in glory (Matt 24:30).

Jesus taught that those who would be part of God's Kingdom must live according to standards that surpassed even those of the Law of Moses as it was commonly interpreted (cf. Matt 5:17–48). The laws of Moses allowed a person to take vengeance against those who had injured them; the teachings of Jesus urged non-retaliation (Matt 5:38–42; Luke 6:26–29). The Mosaic laws forbade adultery; Jesus condemned even lusting after another's spouse (Matt 5:27–30). The Mosaic laws permitted divorce with some liberality; Jesus argued that God ideally wanted couples to remain together for life (Matt 5:31–32, 19:3–9; Mark 2:10–12; Luke 16:18). Furthermore, Jesus' interpretations of the law were often at odds with the current ideas of the religious establishment. While many religious groups of the day were scrupulously concerned with the proper observance of the Sabbath or ritual washing of the hands, Jesus tended to downplay or even despise such external observances (e.g., Matt 15:1–20; Mark 3:1–5). Instead, he emphasized the areas that were of deep concern to the Old Testament prophets whose mantle he had taken up: justice, mercy, and a humble attitude toward God and others.

Another important aspect of Jesus' teaching was his self-understanding. Many Gospel passages depict Jesus speaking of himself and his unique relationship to his Father in Heaven.[2] One of the most im-

---

1. The phrases "Kingdom of God" and "Kingdom of Heaven" are synonymous. In Jesus' time, the word "Heaven" was often substituted for the word "God" in order to show reverence for the Almighty. We still do this today, as someone might say, "Heaven help us" instead of "God help us."

2. Since the Gospels were used as textbooks to teach Christian doctrine in the early church, most scholars believe that the Gospels preserve both records of what Jesus

portant affirmations he made about himself was that he was the Messiah, or in the Greek of the New Testament, the Christ. "Messiah" is a title derived from the Hebrew word *mashiach*, which means "anointed one." This word was used by the Jewish people of Jesus' day as a title for the prophesied savior-king who would restore Israel and lead God's people in the ways of truth and justice. Jesus' understanding of the role of the Messiah, however, was likely quite different from that of many of his contemporaries, since he believed in a Kingdom that would be established through spiritual rather than political power. It may be for this reason that Jesus rarely called himself "the Messiah," preferring the more humble title "Son of Man," which simply means "human being."

The Gospels also refer to Jesus as the "Son of God." The significance of this title in the Gospels is somewhat ambivalent. In the Old Testament, the epithet "son of God" or "God's/my son" was applied to angels (e.g., Gen 6:1), Israel (Hos 11:1), or the king of Israel (2 Sam 7:14). As a title for the king, it implied a special relationship between God and his chosen representative, not necessarily any kind of biological relationship. In Luke 1:32, however, this title is connected with Jesus' supernatural conception. Being fathered by the Holy Spirit, he is uniquely "Son of God." Jesus is rarely depicted in the Gospels applying this title to himself (but see John 10:36), but the phrase is often found on the mouths of angels, demons, and God himself (e.g., Matt 4:3, 8:29; Luke 1:32). Apparently, the ability to recognize this aspect of Jesus' character required supernatural insight. But at his trial, Jesus admitted before the high priest that he was "the Messiah, the Son of the Blessed One" (Mark 14:61).

It is in John's Gospel where the divinity of Jesus is most thoroughly explored. Here, Jesus says explicitly that he and the Father are one (John 10:30), and that anyone who has seen him has seen the Father, as well (John 14:9). John includes many statements where Jesus talks of his role as the giver of eternal life (John 3:16; 5:25; 6:35; 11:25), and the only way to the Father (John 14:6). For the Gospel writers, the identity of Jesus was as critical an issue as the moral teachings of Jesus—if not more so.

---

taught about himself and the early Church's teachings about Jesus. Therefore, many scholars question whether Jesus actually called himself "Messiah," "Son of God," etc.

JESUS' MIRACLES

But when most people think of Jesus' ministry, they are likely to be intrigued by his miracles even more than his teachings. But while curing the sick and walking on water are surely striking feats, it should be noted that according to the Gospel accounts, Jesus did not perform miracles merely for the sake of making an impression. While some of his healing miracles were simply motivated by compassion (Matt 14:14), they generally served as signs of the coming of God's Kingdom (John 12:37). Some Jewish teachers in Jesus' day taught that the Old Testament prophets had predicted that the Messiah would perform just such wonders as Jesus did (see, e.g., Isa 61:1-2). And so, when John the Baptist was imprisoned, he sent his disciples to ask Jesus if he was truly the Messiah. Jesus replied, "Go back and tell John what you have seen and heard: the blind see, the lame walk, the lepers are cured, the deaf hear, the dead are raised and the poor have the good news preached to them" (Luke 7:22; cf. Luke 4:17-20). Demon exorcisms, too, were powerful demonstrations that the kingdom of the Devil had met its match—there was new sheriff in town, and he was taking no prisoners!

The most remarkable of Jesus' miracles, recorded only in the Gospel of John (chapter 11), was the resurrection of his friend Lazarus. Lazarus had been dead and buried for three days when Jesus arrived and asked to be taken to the tomb. When he asked for the stone blocking its entrance to be removed, Lazarus's sisters protested that the body would already be putrefying. Jesus replied that if they would trust him, they would see a demonstration of the power of God. The tomb was opened, and Jesus called for Lazarus to come forth. The dead man arose, alive once again. Jesus demonstrated that he was "the resurrection and the life" (John 11:25), and incited the further wrath of the religious leaders of Judea.

JESUS' ENEMIES

The Gospels record that Jesus' words and deeds made him many enemies. The Pharisees, popular religious leaders of the time, feared Jesus' influence. In their opinion, Jesus was leading the people away from the right path by de-emphasizing strict observance of the laws of Moses. As noted above, Jesus taught that distinctive Jewish practices like keeping the Sabbath day, abstaining from pork, and washing before meals were minor matters compared to works of compassion. The Pharisees, believing that neglect in these practices could actually provoke God to judge the nation, were not above resorting to violence in order to "protect" the people from such heresies (see Mark 3:1–6). But an even more serious threat came from the high priest and other corrupt officials in Jerusalem. Jesus had provoked their wrath by exposing the graft taking place in the Temple courts, where the money changers and animal sellers were taking advantage of those who had come to Jerusalem to offer sacrifices to the Lord (Mark 11:12–18 and parallels passages; John 2:12–17). But this was only part of the problem: for those whose power and position depended on the favor of Rome, the rabble-rousing Galilean preacher was dangerous figure. If Jesus incited the people to revolt against Rome, it could mean the end of Judea and the politicians' positions of wealth and prestige (John 11:49–50).

Jesus was not oblivious to these threats. In his parables and his explicit teachings, he predicted that he would be tried and executed by the Gentiles (see Matt 16:21, 21:33–41). He did not welcome or justify this fate, as if he had a death wish. Rather, he condemned the plot as a grievous (but typical) evil (Luke 13:31–35), and predicted that it would bring judgment on Jerusalem (see Mark 12:1–12). But on the other hand, Jesus also believed that his death was part of God's plan for the salvation of the world. He stated that he had not been forced to sacrifice himself, but that he willingly gave himself for the world (John 10:14–18). His life was to be a "ransom" for those who would believe in him (Mark 10:45; Matt 20:28). And so, as he traveled to Jerusalem in AD 30 to celebrate the Passover, he fully expected it to be his last (Mark 10:32–34).

THE TRIAL AND CRUCIFIXION

And indeed, he was not mistaken. When he entered the city on Palm Sunday, he was hailed as the "Son of David" by adoring crowds that pleaded for him to deliver them from their oppressors ("hosanna" is Aramaic for "deliver us"). But the tide would quickly turn against him. On Thursday, after Jesus had celebrated the Passover feast with his disciples, he went to the Garden of Gethsemane to pray in private. As he petitioned God for strength to endure his coming ordeal, one of his disciples, Judas Iscariot, arrived leading a band of Jesus' enemies. Jesus was arrested and taken to Caiaphas, the high priest. A hastily assembled kangaroo court accused Jesus of plotting to destroy the Temple, but the paid witnesses could not get their stories straight. Finally, Jesus was directly challenged to admit he was the Messiah. He confessed that he was, but added that the priests and council would see Jesus sitting at the right hand of God. To the high priest, this claim constituted blasphemy worthy of death. Jesus was then sent on to the Roman governor Pontius Pilate for an official trial—not for blasphemy, which did not interest Rome, but for sedition. The mercurial governor was initially reluctant to condemn Jesus, but eventually he succumbed to the urging and threats of the local authorities. He ordered Jesus to be executed in the method typically used for insurgents—crucifixion.

Jesus was beaten and mocked before being taken away to a place on the outskirts of the city called Golgotha. There, he was stripped of his clothes and nailed to a cross. A sign was placed on the cross saying, "Jesus of Nazareth, King of the Jews." For several hours he endured the agony and humiliation of crucifixion, while praying for the forgiveness of those who tormented him. But in the late afternoon, as a supernatural darkness hung over the land, Jesus finally died. His body was claimed by some of his followers, who hastily prepared it for burial before the evening, when the Sabbath began. A wealthy disciple, Joseph of Arimathea, placed Jesus in his own newly-dug tomb and sealed it with a stone. The Jewish authorities, fearing that the disciples might attempt to steal Jesus' body, placed guards at the tomb (Matt 25:64–66).

THE RESURRECTION

But the story of Jesus was not yet complete. On the third day after his crucifixion, the women who had gone to re-wrap Jesus' body in proper fashion found that the stone was rolled away from the tomb entrance, and the body of Jesus was missing. An angel informed the women that Jesus had been resurrected from the dead. The Book of Acts states that over the next forty days, he was seen repeatedly by his disciples (Acts 1:3). Jesus ate with them and explained to them from the Scriptures why it was necessary for him to die and be raised again in this manner. Finally, Jesus led his disciples out to the town of Bethany, where was taken up into heaven. But the disciples were left with a promise that Jesus would one day return again from heaven (Acts 1:11).

The biblical account of Jesus' life, death, and resurrection is straightforward enough for a Sunday school child to appreciate, and yet it is deep enough to fully engage the attention of biblical scholars and theologians. In the chapters that follow, we will explore Jesus' historical and cultural context. Perhaps even those who have known and loved his story for years will discover a new appreciation for Jesus as a man of his times, and a Man for all times.

2

Windows into the Past

Reconstructing the world of Jesus can be tricky business. We cannot transport ourselves to ancient Judea and observe daily life and historical events as they occur, getting a flawless picture of what Jesus did and why he did it. Instead, our view of the world of Jesus must be reconstructed from sources that have survived the last two thousand years. The artifacts we have at our disposal are like little windows into the past. Unfortunately, these windows are never large enough to give us a full picture, and rarely located where we wish they were. In fact, given the bias and selectivity of our sources, we might say that they were originally composed of fractured bits of stained glass, rather than clear window panes. Furthermore, they are now covered with dust accumulated through the passing centuries. The images we can discern are partial and distorted, and cannot be deciphered without a good deal of creative interpretation.

We can divide our sources into two categories: the physical evidence and the textual evidence. Physical evidence consists of artifacts and ruins unearthed by archeological excavations. Textual evidence is the documents left behind by ancient people. Both sources have their strengths and their weaknesses. Sometimes, they corroborate each others' testimony; sometimes, they contradict one another. And most often, the relationship between the sources is difficult to interpret. Many a scholarly battle has been waged over the relative weight to be given to physical and textual witnesses in reconstructing the past.

THE PHYSICAL EVIDENCE

If we could believe Hollywood, archeologists would seem to be an adventurous lot. Booby-trapped tombs, ancient curses, priceless artifacts buried under mounds of rubble—it all looks very romantic through the magic eye of the movie camera. But of course, real archeologists are about as different from Indiana Jones as ballet is from break dancing. They rarely get rich, seldom make headlines, and are much more adept with a trowel and brush than a bull whip. And yet, archeology has proven an invaluable aid to biblical scholars. Time and again, difficult passages have been illuminated or uncertain episodes substantiated by the fortuitous turn of the excavator's spade.

While people have been digging up ruins from time immemorial, archeology as a science is a relatively young discipline. In the centuries past, people who explored ancient palaces and tombs were mostly interested in finding treasures that they could sell to museums, collectors, or—worst of all!—for salvage, to be reused as raw materials. There was little systematic investigation of sites, little effort to document procedures or findings, and little concern about preserving items that the excavators found unattractive or uninteresting. Even as late as the nineteenth century, archeology was still in a barbaric state. In the 1870's when Heinrich Schliemann excavated Troy, he plowed through layers of artifacts, heedless of the destruction he was causing. He was convinced that the deepest layer of the settlement would be the Troy described by Homer in his great work, the Iliad, and uncovering the legendary city was really all that interested him. Once he reached the lowest habitation levels of the site, he sorted through the debris looking for evidence linking the site to characters or episodes from Homer's narrative. In actuality, he had dug right through the Troy of King Priam's day, and doubtless destroyed many priceless relics in the process. Because of such work as this, many physical remains from the ancient world have been lost forever.

Modern archeologists are far more careful and systematic. They pay close attention to soil layers (stratigraphy) in order to have a good idea of the relative ages of materials they uncover. They carefully document where each item is found and its relationship to other artifacts and adjacent structures. Items are photographed *in situ* and excavated with painstaking care. These procedures have yielded some remarkable results for the time of Jesus. We have learned many interesting facts about daily life in Bible times. In fact, since the literature of the time generally focused on the "important" people, the only information we have about the lives of the common people (like Mary and Joseph) comes from archeological remains.

In recent years, there have been numerous significant archeological discoveries of first century artifacts. Masada and Herodium, two fortresses important in the first century AD, have been extensively excavated and have yielded many interesting finds. The site known as Khirbet Qumran, near the hiding places of the Dead Sea Scrolls, has been thoroughly studied, and yet controversy about who inhabited this site in the time of Jesus continues. In a section of Jerusalem known as the "upper city," several private homes from the first century have been discovered, and now serve as a museum where visitors can get a glimpse of the lives of the well-to-do of Jesus' day. Some discoveries have made headlines, including an ossuary (box containing human bones) bearing the (very likely forged) inscription "James the Brother of Jesus." A first-century fishing boat discovered in the Sea of Galilee has caused many to speculate that this could have been the very craft in which Jesus sat while he taught, or where he performed his miracle of calming the storm.[1]

These findings have excited interest and stirred controversy, but in the final analysis, they have done little to increase our knowledge of first-century Galilee and Judea. The fact is, there are limits on the usefulness of archeology for reconstructing ancient Jewish history, for several reasons. To begin with, the most important sites from Palestine have been continuously inhabited from ancient times, and remain so to this day. It is difficult to excavate in places where people are currently living. Furthermore, many of the questions that intrigue us most are precisely the kind of questions archeology cannot answer. For instance, archeological evidence might tell us that there were Roman troops in Syria in 63 BC, but alone, it probably cannot tell us why they were there. In theory, archeologists might be able to show us that the tomb of Jesus is empty. But they could probably not tell us how it came to be that way, or why.

A final weakness of the archeological approach is that ancient artifacts can be difficult to interpret. A small statue may have been an idol that once had a place of honor in an ancient shrine, or it might have been a child's toy. How can we know for sure? Recently, an archeologist in Jerusalem claimed to have found Jesus' family tomb, with the bones of Jesus in it. The appearance of the names "Joseph," "Miriam" (Mary), "Jacob" (James), and "Jesus" inscribed on some of the ossuaries was his

---

1. Many of these recent findings have made their way into the popular press, as in Adler and Underwood, "Search for the Sacred," 37–41.

evidence for identifying the tomb with Jesus of Nazareth.[2] Other competent archeologists quickly pointed out that these were all very common names in Jesus' time. Furthermore, working-class people in those days did not have family tombs—they buried their dead in graveyards. And finally, even if Jesus' family did have a tomb, it would have been located in Galilee, where Jesus' family actually lived, not in Jerusalem where he died. Artifacts can sometimes be the academic equivalent of Rorschach ink blots, telling us more about the state of mind of the archeologist than the ancient world.

So as interesting and exciting as archeology might be, we depend far more heavily on textual evidence for reconstructing the history and culture of Jesus' world. And so we will turn our attention now to that topic.

THE CLASSICAL AUTHORS

When scholars want to reconstruct the history of the classical (ancient Greek and Roman) world, they depend heavily on the works of the Greek and Roman historians. For the centuries before the time of Jesus, the most important of these historians are the Greek writers Herodotus (ca. 484-425 BC), who wrote a history of the wars between the Greeks and Persians, and Thucydides (460-395 BC), who wrote an account of the struggle between Athens and Sparta. Thucydides has often been called the father of modern history because he claimed to have written an objective account, to have rejected myths and legends, and to have interviewed as many eyewitnesses as possible. His work became the model that subsequent writers tried to copy.

These writers provide us with some important Bible background, especially significant for reconstructing the context of the Intertestamental Period (the time between the end of the Old Testament and the beginning of the New Testament). But they are of little help for reconstructing events of New Testament times, since they died long before Jesus was born. For the events of Jesus' day, we must look to later classical historians. One of the most important of these is the Roman writer Gaius Suetonius Tranquillus (ca. AD 70-140), usually referred to simply as Suetonius. His *Lives of the Caesars*, published around AD 120, summarizes the careers of all the Roman emperors up to his day. While this work tells us much

---

2. Jacobovici and Pellegrino, *The Jesus Family Tomb*. For a more balanced perspective, see Evans, *Jesus and the Ossuaries*.

about the administration of the Roman Empire, it has little to say about affairs in so unimportant a realm as Palestine. It does, however, contain a tantalizing reference to a disturbance that occurred in Rome in AD 49, when the Emperor Claudius expelled the Jews from Rome because of a trouble maker called Chrestus (*Claudius*, xxv). Many scholars believe that this "Chrestus" is probably a mistaken rendering of "Christus," or Christ. Suetonius could well be reporting a case of tensions in the Jewish community of Rome due to Christian-Jewish rivalry.

Another important Roman historian was Cornelius Tacitus (ca. AD 56–120). His most important works include the *Histories*, which covers Roman events in the period from AD 69 to AD 96, and the *Annals*, which cover AD 14–68. Neither work has survived intact, but the portions that have come down to us are considered among the most important sources for Roman history in this era. Like Suetonius, however, Tacitus has little interest in Judean events. His most direct references to Jesus appear in his account of the burning of Rome in AD 69, a disaster that the Emperor Nero had pinned on the Christians. Tacitus observes only that the Christians were founded by "Christ," who had been "executed in the reign of Tiberius by the procurator Pontius Pilate" (*Annals* 15.44.3).

There are a few other classical authors who make similarly brief references to Jesus and his times. Pliny the Younger (ca. AD 61–113), a Roman writer who once served as a governor in Asia Minor (modern Turkey), wrote about Christians of his day who worshipped Christ as a god (Book 10, Letter 96), but he has little to say about Jesus himself. An author named Thallos, whose three-volume history of the eastern Mediterranean has mostly perished, made what is probably the earliest surviving reference to Jesus outside of the New Testament. According to the Christian historian Georgius Syncellus, in AD 55, Thallos attempted to explain away the mysterious darkness that fell on the afternoon of Jesus' crucifixion as a solar eclipse.[3]

All in all, the classical sources tell us a great deal about the Roman world in which Jesus lived, but little about Jesus, or even Palestine. And while that fact may be disappointing, it is not especially surprising. The affairs of Galilee and Judea could hardly be of any interest to the people of Rome, who generally regarded anyone but the Greeks as contempt-

---

3. As Julius Africanus noted in AD 220, this explanation does not hold water: Jesus was crucified during the Feast of Passover, which always coincided with the full moon. Solar eclipses cannot occur during the time of the full moon.

ible. So if we truly want to understand the history and culture of the Jews, we have to look to the Jewish authors themselves.

THE APOCRYPHA

Several Jewish writers have provided invaluable information about the history and culture of Palestine around the time of Jesus. Some of this literature has been preserved in the Apocrypha (Greek for "hidden"), a collection of Jewish texts that have been included in Catholic and Orthodox versions of the Old Testament, but usually excluded from Protestant versions. The books of the Apocrypha were originally written in Hebrew, Aramaic, and Greek, and date from the fourth century BC to the first century AD. These texts were apparently read as Scripture by some Jewish communities, but apparently not among the Jews in Palestine. They are never quoted in the New Testament, and Jewish writers from around the time of Jesus do not seem to regard them as Scripture. Nonetheless, they were translated into Greek (the common language of the Mediterranean region for several centuries before the time of Jesus) and preserved among the Jews of the *Diaspora*, or "dispersion" (the Jews living outside Palestine). As Christianity spread throughout the Roman Empire, the Church adopted books of the Apocrypha as part of their Bible, but rabbinic Judaism officially rejected them as uninspired and non-scriptural.

The reasons these books are not included in Protestant Bibles are complex. To begin with, some important Church Fathers—most notably, Origen, Tertullian, and Jerome—had already challenged the authority of the apocryphal books in the early centuries of the Church age. Jerome is particularly important in this regard, since he was commissioned to produce an authoritative Latin translation of the Bible for use in the Church. While Jerome argued that these books could be edifying reading, he insisted they should not be the basis for authoritative doctrines of the Church. In the common mind, however, it was impossible to wholly separate between "edifying reading" and Scripture. Since the books of the Apocrypha were included in Latin translations of the Old Testament, they were read in the churches and in devotions as if they were Bible. In the fifteenth century, when the Protestant reformers were creating translations of the Scriptures in English and German so that Christians could read the Bible in their own languages, they sought to use the best manuscripts possible. For the Old Testament, they determined that the

Hebrew text of the Jewish scribes was superior to the Greek translations used in the Church. Since the texts of the Apocrypha were mostly translations, not originals, the Reformers (citing Saint Jerome) determined that they could not be considered trustworthy. They also had theological reasons for rejecting these books, since the Catholic Church used passages from the Apocrypha to support some beliefs (such as Purgatory) that the Protestants rejected. Often, the books of the Apocrypha were included between the Old and New Testaments in Protestant translations, but with a note that they were not to be considered authoritative Scripture.

The contents of the Apocrypha vary between Catholic and Orthodox traditions, with the Orthodox Bibles generally including a few more books than the Catholic. They represent a variety of literary types: Tobit and Judith are heroic tales, the Wisdom of Solomon and Ben Sira are collections of proverbs, the two Books of Maccabees are historical in nature. Several other texts are additions to existing biblical texts. These include additions to Esther that give the book a decidedly more religious feel, stories about Daniel that emphasize the hero's God-given cleverness at solving riddles and frustrating evil doers, a letter by the prophet Jeremiah, and an additional Psalm. There are also texts that represent what is sometimes called "rewritten Bible," retellings of biblical stories that are meant to bring out specific theological or ethical lessons.

Since they derive from the time that Protestants have traditionally deemed "the four hundred silent years" (the intertestamental period), the books of the Apocrypha can shed interesting light on an era that is passed over in many Bibles. They serve as an important bridge between the Israelite religion of the Old Testament and the Jewish religion of Jesus' day. Many New Testament ideas that are absent or downplayed in the Old Testament (e.g., the afterlife, angels and demons, personal piety) play important roles in these stories. But when it comes to our understanding of intertestamental *history*, the books of 1 and 2 Maccabees are among our most important sources. Unlike, say, 1 and 2 Kings, which present two consecutive eras of Israel's history, these two books cover pretty much the same period of time, beginning with Antiochus Epiphanes' persecution of the Jews in 167 BC and going up to the early days of the Hasmonean dynasty (see Chapter 4). Their difference is mostly one of perspective. First Maccabees was originally written in Hebrew or Aramaic, and is patterned after the biblical books of the

Kings; Second Maccabees was originally written in Greek, and includes elements that might be considered "fantastic" or "sensational." Together, these books provide invaluable information on one of the most crucial eras of Jewish history.

THE PSEUDEPIGRAPHA AND DEAD SEA SCROLLS

Outside of the Apocrypha, there were a great many other Jewish religious texts from the intertestamental era that have been passed on to us in various forms. These works are collectively known as the "pseudepigrapha" (the singular form is pseudepigraphon, meaning "false ascription"). The pseudepigrapha were compositions written in the names of long-dead saints. Usually they were prophetic in nature, with the departed holy men "predicting" events that were occurring in the actual author's own day, and asserting through divine revelation how those events would conclude. The First Book of Enoch, which is quoted in the New Testament (Jude 14), is the most famous of these works. Although it is written in the name of the saint mentioned in Genesis 5:18–23, most scholars agree that 1 Enoch is actually a compilation of texts composed in the first and second centuries BC. The best manuscripts of this text are preserved in the Ethiopic language, although some Aramaic language fragments have been found among the Dead Sea Scrolls. There were also pseudepigrapha that were more "didactic" in nature. The Book of Jubilees, for instance, is presented as a revelation given to Moses, but it is clearly designed to instruct Jews of the Greek era in how they should relate to their Gentile neighbors.

We might find this kind of literature troubling today. In fact, some would call it outright dishonest. It must be borne in mind, however, that these texts were written for the purposes of encouraging and exhorting people to remain true to their faith, especially in times of trouble. The authors were not bad people. They were using a literary technique that was widely employed in that day, just as a modern novelist might put him or herself in the persona of a historical or fictional character in order to tell their story in a more vivid manner.

Many of the pseudepigrapha, previously known only in Greek versions or other ancient translations, are now known (at least in part) in their original Hebrew and Aramaic versions due to the discovery of the Dead Sea Scrolls. The Dead Sea Scrolls are ancient Jewish manuscripts (hand-written copies) dating from about 200 BC to around AD

70. The first of the scrolls were discovered in 1947 in a cave near the Dead Sea. Over the next couple decades, more scrolls were discovered in other caves. In all, about 30,000 fragments of manuscripts have been discovered, which if fully assembled would comprise between 800 and 900 texts. Unfortunately, most of the texts are very fragmentary, having been damaged by the ravages of time and sometimes by the efforts of local scroll-hunters.

The vast majority of the Scrolls could be loosely called religious, although a few private documents and lists appear among them, as well. About two hundred of the texts are manuscripts of books of the Hebrew Bible, the oldest known copies of the Old Testament in existence. About fifty texts represent books of the Apocrypha and pseudepigrapha previously known from translations: e.g., the Wisdom of Ben Sira; Tobit; the First Book of Enoch; Jubilees. Then, there are religious texts that were completely new to us. Many of these derive from a group that called itself the "Community," a religious association that came into being in the days before Jesus and may have existed contemporaneously with him. Led by "the Righteous Teacher," this group was persecuted by the religious establishment in Jerusalem and forced to flee to "the wilderness of Damascus," where they re-established their community. Many scholars believe they eventually settled at the site known as Khirbet Qumran by the Dead Sea, although this theory has had numerous detractors. Often, the Community is identified with the Essenes, a Jewish sect described by ancient historians (see Chapter 7).

The Dead Sea Scrolls comprise one of our best resources for reconstructing the religious and cultural setting of Jesus' day. In them, we see reflected the diversity and intolerance that characterized Judaism in this period. We also find that many of the controversies recorded in the Gospels were indeed live issues for Jewish society of the day. One text, called *Miqsat Ma'aseh Hattorah* ("Some of the Matters of the Law," abbreviated 4QMMT), is a letter written to some figure of political authority. In this letter, the Community presents its disputes with the Jerusalem religious establishment. The sect claims that the leaders in Jerusalem are endangering the entire nation by such practices as improperly washing their hands and allowing lame people into the Temple precincts. With such scruples as these, it is no wonder that Jesus offended the "teachers of the Law" with his relaxed approach to religious ritual.

RABBINIC JUDAISM

Rabbinic Judaism refers to the form of Jewish religion that came into prominence in the third century AD, and has continued to develop until the present day. We will only briefly consider the most important texts of Rabbinic Judaism, the Mishnah and the Talmud. The Mishnah ("second" [law?]) is a collection of oral laws assembled around AD 240. The earliest of these regulations could well go back to the time of Jesus, while the latest date to the third century AD. They cover a wide variety of issues, such as ritual bathing, Sabbath observance, tithing, and other distinctive Jewish practices. These traditions are arranged according to subject into six major divisions, such as *Zeraim* ("seeds"; traditions dealing with agricultural laws and food regulations), *Mo`ed* ("appointed times"; various festivals and other observances), and *Nashim* ("women"; mostly laws dealing with women's issues). Each division further is subdivided into units called "tractates," again titled according to their subject matter: e.g., *Maaseroth* ("tithes"); *Shabbath* ("the Sabbath day"); *Middoth* ("measurements"). Jesus is never mentioned in the Mishnah, although there may be some oblique references to Christians in passages that discuss the teachings of "sectarians." The Mishnah demonstrates the kind of legal issues and methods of argumentation that may have occupied the Pharisees of Jesus' day. But since it is so far removed from the first century, and since it often seems to represent ideals rather than practical instruction, its usefulness for reconstructing first century history and religion is dubious.

The Talmud ("teaching") consists of the Mishnah plus the commentary of later rabbis. There are actually two editions, a "Palestinian" or "Jerusalem Talmud" (abbreviated *y.* for "Yerushalmi," the Aramaic spelling of Jerusalem), collated in the fourth century AD, and the "Babylonian Talmud" (abbreviated *b.*), probably from the early seventh century. It is the Babylonian Talmud that people refer to when they speak of "the Talmud," since it is the version Orthodox Jews consider authoritative. Both texts are fascinating reading, often including imaginative stories and parables designed to illustrate points of law or theology. Since Christianity was so prominent in the days of the Talmud, it is not surprising to find references here to Christians and to Jesus. Nor is it surprising that these references are seldom sympathetic. Talmudic tradition identifies Jesus as the illegitimate son of a Roman soldier named Pantera (*b. Shabb.* 104b). He fled to Egypt during the days of King

Alexander Janneus (*b. Sanh.* 107b).⁴ He was arrested by the Jews because he practiced sorcery, and when after forty days no one was found to speak in his defense, he was hung (*b. Sanh.* 43a-b). Jesus is punished in Hell by being tortured with boiling excrement (*b. Git.* 57a). The story is an obvious parody of the Christian gospel, and should not be used for reconstructing the historical circumstances of Jesus' life or ministry.

While the Mishnah and Talmud may record some authentic traditions from the first century, they should not be considered reliable sources for historical or cultural information about the time of Jesus. Not only are they several centuries removed from Jesus' day, they also freely employ idealization and imaginative reconstructions as teaching tools.

PHILO OF ALEXANDRIA AND FLAVIUS JOSEPHUS

There are two early Jewish writers to whom we owe an incalculable debt. The first of these is Philo of Alexandria, also known as Philo Judeus. Philo was probably born sometime around 20 BC, and he lived until sometime after AD 40. He was an aristocratic Jew from Alexandria, the capital city of Egypt and the center of learning and trade in the ancient world. Philo was a respected statesman and an extremely productive author. He wrote volumes on philosophy, biblical interpretation, and history, many of which have survived to this day. His philosophical writings represent the first attempt to reconcile Jewish beliefs with the ideas of contemporary philosophers, and served as a model for later Christian philosophers. His methods of biblical interpretation, too, deeply influenced some of the early Church fathers. These included Origen, who emulated Philo's method of reading Old Testament stories as theological allegories. And as a historian, Philo recorded not only important political events, but also provided useful descriptions of Jewish customs and beliefs in his day. Unfortunately, he has nothing directly to say about Jesus, and in fact tells us little about Palestinian Judaism.

Philo's value to the historian pales in comparison to that of our foremost source on Judaism in the time of Jesus: Flavius Josephus. Josephus was born about AD 37 to an aristocratic Judean Jewish family. He claims to have excelled in learning and piety, exploring the various Jewish religious sects before becoming a Pharisee. As a young man, he was sent

---

4. In reality, Alexander Janneus died about seventy years before Jesus was born.

with a delegation to Rome to help negotiate the release of some Jewish priests imprisoned there. When he returned home in AD 67, Judea was in revolt against the Romans. Though still young, Josephus was given responsibility for organizing the defense of Galilee. But when the Roman troops advanced on his army, most of Josephus's men deserted. Josephus took refuge with the remnants of his army in the city of Jotapata, but after a siege, the Romans breached the city's defenses. Josephus and forty of his men fled to a cave, where they made a suicide pact, preferring death to capture. But Josephus was opposed to the idea, and after his comrades had all killed themselves, he surrendered to the enemy. Josephus ingratiated himself to the Roman general Vespasian by arguing that he could be useful in persuading the Jews to surrender. Furthermore, he claimed to be a skilled interpreter of prophecy, and predicted to Vespasian that the general would one day become the emperor of Rome. It seemed like an unlikely development at the time, since Nero was the current emperor, and Vespasian was not related to him in any way. But when Nero was assassinated without leaving an heir, and his successor quickly succumbed to the same fate, Vespasian was selected by the legions to be the leader of the Roman Empire. Josephus was given quarters in the Emperor's palace and a government pension. He then proceeded to write his memoirs, as well as several other works designed to present the Jews in a positive light before the Greco-Roman world.

Josephus composed his historical works at the end of the first century AD. The first was an account of the war against Rome called *The Jewish War*, written ca. AD 79. The other surviving works were all written in the last decade of the first century AD. His autobiography, *The Life of Flavius Josephus*, is the earliest surviving autobiographical memoir. It gives a somewhat different account of his role in the Revolt than what we find in *The Jewish War*. An apologetic work entitled *Against Apion* was designed to defend Judaism against its detractors. But his largest work was the historical survey entitled *The Antiquity of the Jews*. This book covered the history of the Jewish people from Adam to his own day. He gives us little information about the Old Testament era that we do not learn from the Bible itself, but for the intertestamental period, he obviously had access to sources that no longer exist today. Some of his reports are clearly legendary; some are a mix of legend and history; some are his own creations. Much of his information, however, seems quite reliable, deriving from official reports and histories that have long perished. For the time of Jesus, his detailed reports on Jewish politics and religion are especially valuable.

For most of the last 2,000 years, Jewish scholars have tended to despise Josephus as a traitor to his people, while Christian scholars have held his work in esteem. It was Christian scribes who preserved his writings through the years, and they occasionally could not resist the urge to "improve" his text in various ways. This tendency is evident in his brief description Jesus' ministry, the so-called *Testimonium Flavianum*:[5]

> About this time there was a wise man, Jesus—if it be right to call him a man. For he was a worker of amazing deeds, a teacher of those who receive truth with pleasure, and he won over many Jews, along with many of the Greeks. This one was the Christ. Upon the accusation of our leading men, Pilate condemned him to the cross; but those who first loved him did not cease. For on the third day he appeared to them alive again, the divine prophets having prophesied these and a myriad other things about him. Until now, the tribe of Christians, so named for him, has not disappeared.

Scholars have devoted a good deal of attention to this passage. As it stands now, it almost reads as if Josephus were a Christian, which is highly unlikely in light of his other works. Most scholars are convinced the current text is the product of a Christian copyist. But what, if anything, did Josephus actually write about Jesus? Some scholars see the entire passage as a fabrication, but most agree that at least part of it is authentic. Given the attention that Christianity was receiving in the later decades of the first century AD, it would have been strange for Josephus to have passed over Jesus without mention. Also, it seems unlikely that a Christian scribe would refer to the Church as "the tribe of Christians." We very likely have some genuine words of Josephus here, heavily edited for Christian consumption. We can be fairly sure that Josephus did not say that Jesus was the Christ, but he may have said, "He was *called* the Christ." He probably did not say that Jesus appeared alive again, but is it possible that he said that the Christians *claimed* that Jesus appeared alive? Scholars have suggested a number of other reconstructions, based in part on whether they believe Josephus would have held a negative, positive, or neutral opinion of Jesus.

---

5. *Ant.* 18:63–64.

Whatever we make of the *Testimonium*, we cannot deny the usefulness of Josephus's writings for understanding early Jewish history and culture. Today, even his harshest critics acknowledge the debt we owe to this Jewish general/traitor/apologist. Josephus must be read with a critical eye: his reports are not unbiased. He was very egotistical by modern standards, and he sometimes projected his own ideas and experiences on to his subject matter. His retellings of the biblical stories reveal some of his other tendencies. In order to defend his people against accusations that the Jews were a new people on the world scene who had never accomplished anything of note, Josephus often "embellishes" the biblical narratives to depict the Jewish people as even more ancient and noble than they actually were. (In Josephus's account, Abraham taught mathematics and astrology to the Egyptians!) He also highlights in his biblical paraphrases how the Jews are ideal subjects of foreign powers. And in his accounts of the Jewish revolt, Josephus tried to place the blame for the war on the low-class rabble, while he cast himself and other members of the upper classes in the best possible light. These books are, to an extent, propaganda. But when read with a critical eye, they are unparalleled witnesses to the history and culture of the Jewish people.

CHRISTIAN WRITINGS

We would of course expect Christian writers to take more interest in the life and ministry of Jesus than Jews or pagans would, and we shall not be disappointed. The early Christian writings provide numerous stories relating to Jesus' youth and ministry, and record a great many sayings of Jesus (called *agrapha*, "not written") that were not found in the canonical Gospels. The value of these traditions for reconstructing the historical circumstances of Jesus' ministry, however, has been much debated.

The earliest of the Church Fathers' writings date from the second century AD. Being so close to Jesus' day, we might assume that these texts give an accurate reflection of his life and times. But unfortunately, this presumption is probably wrong. First of all, these Church Fathers are not from Palestinian Jewish backgrounds. They are all Gentiles, usually from the cosmopolitan centers of the Roman Empire. By the second century AD, animosity between the Jews and the Church leadership was already intense. The Church Fathers reflected the general anti-Jewish sentiment of their times, and they demonstrate little interest in exploring Jesus' cultural roots. Most of the stories and sayings attributed to

Jesus are patently absurd. And even those saying that appear possibly authentic on the surface have not held up well to scrutiny. Scholars investigating the *agrapha* have determined that very few of these sayings (if any) are true remembrances of Jesus' words and deeds. Many of them are what we might term glosses (interpretive expansions) on the Gospels. For example, after relating the story of the rich ruler who came to Jesus to inquire how he could have eternal life, the agraphon called *The Gospel According to the Hebrews* adds, "How can you say, 'I have kept the Law and the Prophets'? For it is written in the Law, 'You shall love your neighbor as yourself.' And behold, many of your brothers, sons of Abraham, are clad in filth, dying of hunger, and your house is full of many good things, and nothing at all goes out of it to them."[6] Other passages are simply paraphrases or garbled versions of teachings recorded in the canonical Gospels. Examples include, "I am the true gate," and "Do not call anyone on earth your father."[7]

The texts discovered at Nag Hammadi in Egypt have sometimes been cited as evidence for the historical Jesus. These texts were produced by Gnostics, a branch of Christianity deemed heretical by the early Church. Gnosticism was a diverse movement, but generally it tended to downplay Jesus' humanity and sought salvation through revelation and union with Jesus' spiritual nature. The Gnostic texts, especially the pseudepigraphic Gospel of Thomas, have received much media attention, and some scholars have even proposed that they should have equal footing with the canonical Gospels as witnesses to the historical Jesus. But given their late date (mid- to late- second century AD and beyond), their obvious dependence on the canonical texts, and their theological purpose, it is certain that these texts are much more valuable for the light they shed on Church history rather than the life and times of Jesus.

THE LETTERS OF PAUL

But of course, when it comes to information about the life and ministry of Jesus, there are no sources that match the documents of the New Testament. Since they are all written in the first century, and most can be confidently ascribed to Jews familiar with Palestinian Jewish history

---

6. This excerpt is preserved in the writings of the Church Father Origen, *On Matthew* 15:14.

7. Hippolytus *Refutation* 5.8.20; Clement *Ecologue of the Prophets* 20.

and culture, the New Testament texts are our most reliable resources. Certainly, they are written primarily for theological purposes rather than historical purposes. But nonetheless, they preserve many details about customs and ideas circulating among the early Jews—details that are frequently corroborated by other ancient historians or archeological evidence.

The earliest references to the life of Jesus in any existing texts come from the letters of St. Paul. His writings bear witness to the basic accounts found in the Gospels: Jesus was descended from King David (Rom 1:7); he was born of a woman (Gal 4:4); he was an authoritative teacher (1 Cor 7:10, 9:14, 11:23–26); he gathered a circle of disciples (Gal 2:9); he attributed symbolic significance to his last Passover meal (1 Cor 11:23–25); he was betrayed (1 Cor 11:23); he was persecuted by Jewish leadership (1 Thess 2:14–16); he was crucified (Gal 3:13; 1 Cor 1:17; Phil 2:8); he was resurrected from the dead on the third day (1 Cor 15:4); he was seen by witnesses (1 Cor15:6–7); he ascended to heaven (Phil 2:9); he promised to come again (1 Thess 4:13–17). More details can be found in the Catholic Epistles (the New Testament letters not composed by Paul), but it is questionable if these texts are earlier or independent of the canonical Gospel accounts. Instead, these texts probably derived their information on Jesus from the Gospels themselves.

THE GOSPELS

The Gospels, while never intended to be "blow-by-blow" accounts of Jesus' life and ministry, nevertheless fill out this picture substantially. Undoubtedly they were designed to do just that: to provide converts to the faith with fuller, authoritative accounts of Jesus' words and deeds. Each account has its own particular emphases. They are not designed to refute one another, but probably circulated in different regions and communities before they were brought together in the New Testament.

The first three Gospels, Matthew, Mark, and Luke, present a very similar picture of Jesus. These three are collectively known as the "Synoptic" Gospels, from the Greek word meaning "seen together." Most scholars consider these texts to be more historically accurate than John's account, which is regarded as more theological. In fact, the Jesus Seminar, a group of investigators who meet regularly to discuss the historicity of the Gospel accounts, literarily deems none of the sayings in John's Gospel to be authentic words of Jesus. Rather, they argue that these words are the creation of a later community of believers seeking to present the Church's theology in narrative form. But on the other hand, there are scholars who point out that John's descriptions of some geographical features of Jerusalem have been corroborated by archeology (e.g., the pool near the Sheep Gate [5:2] and the place of judgment [19:13]). His knowledge of Jewish customs, too, seems impressive. While John's Gospel surely incorporates more theological reflection than the others, its historical value is hardly negligible.

The origins of the Gospels have also been a topic of extensive debate. Traditionally, they were assigned to the apostles and others whose names they bear: Matthew the apostle; John Mark, disciple of Peter and traveling companion of Barnabas; Luke, companion of St. Paul; and the apostle John. But in actuality, none of the Gospels are actually "signed" by their authors. The earliest manuscripts are all anonymous. Our bases for their attributions are some well attested statements from the early Church Fathers. So while the attributions are not original, they are ancient. And of course, the Gospels themselves are more ancient still. Not produced generations after the time of Jesus as skeptics sometimes claim, there is abundant evidence that the Gospels were all produced in their current form within decades of Jesus' ministry. All four of the canonical Gospels are mentioned in writings of the Church Fathers that date from the early second century AD. The oldest existing Gospel fragment, the Rylands papyrus (P52), is a portion of a copy of John's Gospel. It is usually dated around AD 125. And since it is a copy, we can be assured that the original Gospel of John was more ancient still. Furthermore, John is usually considered the latest of the Gospels—the others are probably even closer to the events they record.

What sources did the Gospel writers use for their compositions? Did they depend solely on oral tradition, or did they use written documents, as well? Since the three Synoptic Gospels often reproduce each other's episodes almost verbatim, most scholars believe that there are common written sources underlying these three accounts. The most widely accepted theory for the relationship between them is called the "two source hypothesis." According to this theory, Mark, the shortest of the Gospels, was written first. Since many of the stories in Matthew and Luke are almost word-for-word identical to those in Mark, it is believed that Matthew and Luke used Mark as one of their sources. But Matthew and Luke also include many sayings of Jesus that are not found in Mark (or John either, for that matter). So it has been proposed that Matthew and Luke shared a common source for these sayings: a compendium of Jesus' teachings that has been designated "Q" (from the German word *Quelle*, meaning "source"). It has also been proposed that Matthew and Luke used other sources for their own unique materials. John, it has been argued, used a source document called the "Signs Gospel."

However these books came into being, we are blessed to have four complementary accounts of Jesus' life, death, and resurrection. Each account has its own unique emphases, probably having been written for different audiences. Matthew's Gospel has traditionally been understood to have been addressed to Jewish readers, and indeed, this Gospel seems to bring out aspects of Jesus' ministry that would have intrigued those raised in Judaism: how Jesus fulfilled Old Testament prophecy; his understanding of the Law; his role as the new and greater Moses. Mark's Gospel has traditionally been associated with Rome, and like the great city itself, this account percolates with power. Even though it is the shortest of the Gospels, it includes more miracle and exorcism accounts than any of the others. In Mark, the emphasis is on Jesus' authority. Luke, writing for a Greco-Roman audience, adopts many of the conventions typical of Greek writers of the time. Like many Greek and Roman writers, he addresses his work to a dignitary, though the Gospel is obviously intended for a wider audience (Luke 1:1–4). Like the Greek historian Thucydides, he claims to have investigated his subject carefully and to have depended on eyewitness accounts, not mere hearsay (Luke 1:1–4). His account emphasizes matters of universal appeal in the Hellenistic world: social justice for women, the poor, and the oppressed. John's Gospel is written for the benefit of the early Christians who were beginning to struggle with the issue of Jesus' relationship with God the Father. It is by far the most theological of the Gospel accounts. So we have been given four very different Gospels, but they all reflect different facets of the same Jesus. The various accounts should not be a cause for embarrassment: they bear witness to a man so complex that if we tried to exhaust his story, "even the world itself would not contain the books that would be written" (John 21:25).

3

The Land and Its Peoples

JESUS LIVED AND MINISTERED in a region we now know as "Palestine." On the west, this land is bordered by the Mediterranean Sea; on the east, by the Jordan River. It stretches north to Syria and south to the Sinai Peninsula. At about 45 miles wide east-to-west by 145 miles long north-to-south, it is about the size of the state of Massachusetts. And yet, this little piece of property has often been the crossroads of the world. In Old Testament times, this land was a buffer zone between the two great world powers, Egypt in the south and Mesopotamia in the north. By the time of Jesus, both of these lands had been eclipsed by an even greater power: the Roman Empire. Palestine was no longer the pivot point of the world, and yet it remained a focal point of many of the world's tensions.

The name of this region is somewhat ironic. It originated with the Greeks, who designated the region around the coast "Palestiné," a Greek pronunciation of the word "Philistine." The Philistines had been the ancient arch-enemies of Israel, a people who had entered the Near East as alien invaders in around 1200 BC and settled in the coastlands. By the time of the Persian conquests of the Near East (539 BC) the unique culture and language of the Philistines had all but disappeared, since these immigrants had generally been assimilated to the Semitic culture of their neighbors. But even so, the inhabitants of the historic Philistine cities Ashdod, Ashkelon, and Gaza retained a memory of their heritage. When the Romans took over the region in 63 BC, they adopted the Greek name for the coastal land, calling it (in Latin) Palestina. But it was not until AD 135 that the name was applied to the region including Judea and Galilee. At that time, the Roman Emperor Hadrian, to punish the Jews for revolting against Roman rule, did away with the designations of "Judea" and "Galilee" for the lands of the Jews, and called the entire region "Palestina." Even though the title was inaccurate and actually pejorative, it has stuck through the ages. For our purposes, it is still a convenient title for "the Holy Land" as a geographical region. The term "Judea," as we will see, is not inclusive enough, while the term "Israel" is historically inaccurate, since the geographical region of Palestine actually included Samaria as well—which was very definitely *not* part of Israel.

THE GEOGRAPHY OF PALESTINE

If you landed on the coast of Palestine and began to travel inland, you would find yourself passing through five distinct geographical regions. The coastal plain, once the land of the Philistines (and their northern neighbors the Phoenicians) has a lush Mediterranean climate. The west winds blowing in from the sea provided moisture enough for rich natural vegetation and good harvests of cultivated crops. This region once produced the famed "cedars of Lebanon" that were used to build Solomon's Temple and palace, though no cedars remain there today. Traveling east (inland), the next region is the Shephalah, or foothills. These lowlands were a good place for agriculture and grazing large livestock. In Old Testament times, the Canaanites had inhabited this area. By the time of Jesus, however, there were few Canaanites, their numbers having been extinguished or assimilated to Judea and Samaria.

The next region inland is the hill country, the land originally inhabited by the Israelites. With its rocky, rolling terrain, this land was better suited for grazing flocks of sheep and goats than agriculture. The Israelites employed terrace farming techniques to make this land productive. The elevation here is higher than in the coastal regions or the foothills, with Jerusalem located at 2600 feet above sea level. But as we go further inland, the land begins to fall away, and we enter the region known as the "Judean Wilderness." This far inland, the Mediterranean winds have already deposited all their moisture, so the land is dry and barren. It is quite different from what we might think of as "wilderness": there are no jungles or forests. Indeed, there are few trees at all. It is a forbidding area that seems most suited for growing rocks. Nonetheless, during the rainy season, there is sufficient scrub here for Bedouin to graze their flocks and herds.

The Judean Wilderness is about seven miles across, maintaining a fairly level elevation. But then, the land then drops off precipitously into the region known as the Jordan Valley. The Jordan Valley is part of the Great Rift Valley system, which stretches from Mesopotamia in the north to Africa in the south. But nowhere is it deeper than here, in the environs of Judea. The surface of the Dead Sea, the great lake at the end of the Jordan River, is almost 1300 feet below sea level—the lowest elevation on the surface of the earth. Known in the Bible as the Sea of Arabah or the Salt Sea, the Dead Sea has such a high concentration of minerals—nearly ten times saltier than the oceans—that it can sustain no large life forms. And the land around the Sea is nearly as barren as the waters. Except for a few areas of verdure like Ein Gedi and the Jericho Plain, the landscape here consists of limestone cliffs riddled with caves and a few scrubby plants.

Finally, even though it is not part of Palestine *per se*, we must also mention the land on the east side of the Jordan River, Perea. In Old Testament times, this region encompassed the land known as Gilead. Today, it is part of the Kingdom of Jordan. Perea is Greek for "the other side"; in the New Testament, the area is simply called "the land beyond the Jordan." Extending from the Jordan River about fifteen miles east, in New Testament times, Perea was home of small Jewish settlements which had displaced the earlier inhabitants (mostly Ammonites). This region was rugged, a land of rocks and scrub, and sparsely populated.

Besides these longitudinal regions, the Palestinian terrain also changes significantly as you travel from north to south. The district of Galilee (Hebrew *hag-galil*: "the circuit" or "the district") stretches from Mt. Hermon in the north to Mt. Carmel and Mt. Gilboa in the south. Like the Judean Hill Country further south, it is a generally rocky, semi-mountainous region. Here, however, the hills are quite a bit larger than further south, and the prevailing winds bring in much more moisture than Judea receives. As a result, Galilee has always been a more fertile region than the rest of inland Palestine. On its northwestern boundary, the Plain of Gennesaret produced fruit and vegetables almost all year long. The Sea of Galilee, the setting of much of Jesus' ministry, is actually a freshwater lake about 12 miles long by eight miles wide.

South of Galilee, we come to the land of Samaria. In ancient times, Samaria had been the location of the northern kingdom of Israel. The capital of this kingdom was located in a city called Samaria (1 Kgs 16:24–25). After the kingdom of Israel was destroyed by the Assyrians in 722 BC, the name "Samaria" was applied to the entire region stretching from the Valley of Jezreel on the north to the valley of Aijalon on the south. In New Testament times, it was firmly sandwiched between

Galilee and Judea. Samaria was a hilly land, a fertile place where grains and fruits of all sorts were grown.

South of Samaria was the land known in Jesus' day as "Judea," the Greek rendering of the ancient Hebrew name "Judah." The terrain here was similar to that of Samaria: rocky and hilly. The elevation varies greatly, with peaks reaching as high as 3,000 feet above sea level and deep valleys between them. It was somewhat drier here than it was in Samaria. Indeed, much of Judea could well be considered desert. Olive and fig trees grew here, but little else could grow without extensive cultivation.

THE CLIMATE

Studies have demonstrated that the climate of Palestine has changed very little over the last two thousand years. The weather of today's Israel is much like the weather that Jesus would have experienced. Palestine is located between two distinct climate zones: an arid subtropical region to the south, and a wet subtropical region to the north. There is some considerable regional variation within Palestine itself, based on the amount of rainfall received. Nonetheless, most of the land falls into the typical Mediterranean climate pattern. There are two distinct seasons during the year, a dry season and a wet (or at least wetter) season. There are also seasonal changes in temperature, but these are not as dramatic as the changes in precipitation.

The wet season begins first in the northern regions in about mid October. It ends in the north in about mid-March. The average annual precipitation in Palestine is twenty-two inches, about the same as that of San Francisco, CA. About 70% of the twenty-two inches of precipitation that annually falls in Palestine occurs between the months of November and February, making the region quite dry during the rest of the year. January is the wettest month of the year. On the Coastal Plain, half of the annual rainfall occurs in January, while Jerusalem tends to have a more even distribution of rainfall across the season.

The dry season, beginning in May or June and going through September, can be muggy. The winds coming into Palestine in this period are quite humid, but prevailing atmospheric conditions prevent the formation of rain clouds. There can be stretches of several months that see no rainfall at all.

Temperature variations, while not as significant as the variations in rainfall, are still very noticeable. In December and January, the evening lows can get down to around forty degrees Fahrenheit. It is cool enough for frost, and even occasional snowfalls. Daytime highs will vary from the lower fifties to the lower sixties. In August (middle of the dry season), the temperature rises to an average of 84 degrees in Jerusalem, with the temperature falling off to the mid-sixties in the evening.

THE PRODUCE

Despite its size and less than ideal climate, Palestine managed to have a diverse and productive agricultural industry. The soil had to be thoroughly cultivated and enriched with manure, because it was not especially fertile. But through much hard work and innovation, the Jews and other residents of Palestine caused their land to prosper. Josephus (*War* 3:42–43) tells us that all of Galilee was cultivated. According to the Talmud, this land was rich in grain, wine, figs, vegetables, and fruits. The Sea of Galilee also provided fish for the region. Samaria was also fertile and blessed with rich pastureland (*War* 3:48). Barley and wheat were grown there. Judea was famous for its date palms, which Cleopatra, the queen of Egypt, attempted to seize during the days of King Herod. It also produced a great deal of balsam, a precious spice that brought much income into the country. Olive trees were grown here as well, providing great quantities of the precious oil that was such a staple of ancient Mediterranean society. We know that rice and cotton were cultivated in Palestine in the second century AD, but it is uncertain when these crops were introduced in the land.

THE PEOPLE

The majority population of Palestine in Jesus' day was Jewish. Most of these were Jewish by long ethnic heritage. They could trace their descendants back many generations through their various tribes all the way to Abraham, father of the Israelite people. Many, however, had a more recent association with the Jewish people. Some were members of nations who had been conquered by the Jews in the last couple centuries before the time of Jesus. Under compulsion or by choice, people like the Idumeans (earlier known as the Edomites) in the south and Ammonites to the east had converted to the Jewish faith, and thereby had become part of the Jewish people. Although there was some persistent prejudice against these proselytes, after a few generations they were fully accepted as children of Abraham. They shared the blessings and the stigma (more on this later) of the Jewish race.

In the time of Jesus, there were probably about two million Jews in Palestine, with many more spread throughout the Mediterranean world in what we call the Diaspora ("dispersion"). The Jews of Palestine were concentrated in Judea. Jerusalem was the largest city in Judea, with about 100,000 inhabitants—almost all Jewish. Galilee also had a large Jewish population, although many non-Jewish people lived in this region as well. In Old Testament times, this region was known as "The District of the Nations," and it was mostly populated by non-Israelites. It was conquered by the Jews about 103 BC, and the population forced to convert to Judaism. Also, many residents of Judea moved north to Galilee to take advantage of its more fertile soil. Although there were Gentiles in Galilee in the time of Jesus, recent studies have demonstrated that this region, too, was mostly Jewish.[1] Across the Jordan River, Perea was primarily Jewish, although some non-Jewish cities were located on its borders.

Another large ethnic group in Palestine was the Samaritans. This group, located primarily in Samaria, was surrounded on all sides by the Jews. This arrangement was a source of some considerable discomfort for both parties. The Samaritans were similar in many ways to the Jews: they shared the same Torah, or five Books of Moses; they observed many of the same laws; their sacrificial observances were very like those of the Jews. But the Samaritans were not Jews, ethnically or religiously. Ethnically, the Samaritans claim to be the descendants of the old Israelite tribes of Ephraim and Manasseh. The Old Testament, however, states that the Samaritans originated from non-Israelites who were transported to the region by the Assyrians after they conquered Israel in 721 BC. While the Bible story sounds to some scholars like a "smear campaign" against Judea's archrival, there may be some independent confirmation of the account: Josephus includes a letter in his *Antiquities* Book 12 reputedly written by the Samaritans to a Greek king in which they argue that they are unrelated to the Jews, being descended from the Phoenicians. If the letter is authentic, it would cast doubt on the Samaritans' claim of their descent from Israel. There may be some truth in both stories: the

---

[1]. The evidence has been presented by Chancey, *Myth of a Gentile Galilee*.

Assyrians may well have brought foreigners into the Israelite territory, who then intermarried with the remaining Israelites.

Religiously, the Samaritans differed from the Jews in one primary characteristic: they believed that the Lord should be worshiped not primarily on Mt. Zion in Jerusalem, but on Mt. Gerizim, located in Samaria. This fact accounted for much of the bad blood between the groups. The rest can be accounted for by the fact that the Jews and Samaritans had been fighting with one another since the days of Nehemiah (mid-fifth century BC). These issues will be revisited in Chapter 7.

The Jews and Samaritans were not the only residents of Palestine: there were Syrians as well. The Greeks and Romans broadly applied the title "Syrian" to all the inhabitants of both Syria and Phoenicia. In the New Testament, however, these native Near Easterners are often called "Canaanites." In Jesus' day, many of the Syrians had adopted the characteristics of Greek culture, but there still remained others who spoke the Aramaic language and worshipped their ancestral gods.

Another large ethnic group in Palestine was the Greeks. After Alexander the Great had conquered the East in 332 BC, many Greeks had made their way to various areas in Syria and Palestine to seek their fortune. Alexander's successors had offered financial incentives to encourage Greeks to settle in their territories, creating outposts of reliable allies in their realms. Most of these Greeks had settled in cities established after the models of Greek metropolises. These included a group of cities known as the Decapolis (Greek for "ten cities"), islands of Greek culture located in Galilee and the northern Transjordan region. There were no large Jewish populations in these cities—the presence of so much immorality and idolatry would have been difficult for them to bear.

Finally, by the time of Jesus, there was yet another group of aliens dwelling in Palestine: the Romans. They were not yet numerous in the East. Unlike the Greeks, the Roman Empire did not provide economic incentives for its people to repatriate in the provinces. But the Roman Empire needed soldiers to protect and secure its borders. Most of the Romans in Palestine were just passing though, soldiers or officers fulfilling their duties before returning home to the great modern Italian metropolis. There were also Latin merchants who saw the East as a marvelous marketplace. But there were no Roman cities in Palestine. Only in the Greek-style cities in the East could the Romans feel at home.

CONCLUSIONS

It would probably be accurate to say that the land of Palestine was more diverse geographically than demographically. Although there were people here from all over the Mediterranean world, the population was overwhelmingly Jewish. Truth be told, there was little to draw people to Palestine. Egypt had better farmland. Greece had better schools. Rome had better public works. Palestine was no "Mecca" for the people of the ancient world. It was a place they passed through on the way to something better.

But pass through they did, and their footfalls made deep impressions. As we will see in the next chapter, the many nations and groups that interacted with the Jews and other residents of Palestine influenced the Jews in profound ways—while the Jews would more than return the favor.

4

The Historical Context

THE WORLD INTO WHICH Jesus was born was very different from that of his illustrious ancestor, King David. The mighty powers that had once menaced Israel and Judah—Babylon, Assyria, Egypt, and Persia—were mere shadows of their former glory. Around the Mediterranean Sea, the landscape was shifting westward, and the people of Judea were having a hard time keeping their balance.

THE OLD TESTAMENT BACKGROUND

The story of Israel's origin, its growth to power, and its tragic collapse is told in the Old Testament historical books, beginning in Genesis 12 and stretching through the books of Ezra and Nehemiah. Since this story is familiar from the Bible and will be covered in detail in other volumes of this series, we shall provide here only a brief summary of the biblical account of Israelite history.

In Jesus' day, the Jewish people traced their history back about 2,000 years, to the time of their ancestor Abraham. Abraham had been called by God to establish a nation different from any other in the earth—a nation characterized by its exclusive devotion to the Lord (Yahweh), the "God of the Fathers." God promised Abraham that his descendants would become a great multitude and would inherit the land of Canaan as their own. Abraham's grandson, however, settled his family in Egypt, where they multiplied into the "twelve tribes of Israel." The Egyptians, fearing the growing presence of the Israelites among them, enslaved them for several centuries. Finally (perhaps in 1275 or 1435 BC) the Lord called Moses to deliver the Israelites from Egyptian bondage.[1]

---

1. Those scholars who accept the account of the Exodus as historical are divided on its date. The controversy mainly stems from how literally one should take "400 years" found in Gen 15:13 and Exod 12:40 for the duration of the Israelite sojourn in Egypt.

While camping before a mountain in the Sinai Peninsula, they received the Ten Commandments and other laws that defined the special relationship between Israel and its God.

The Israelites eventually settled into the land we now know as Israel, or more broadly, Palestine (a term we considered in the last chapter). According to the Bible, they displaced or destroyed the earlier inhabitants of the land, the Canaanites, and the various Israelite tribes formed a loose federation. The people were united under the leadership of their first king, Saul, around 1050 BC. Saul, however, was disobedient to God's commands, and was replaced with David, a shepherd from the tribe of Judah. Under David, Israel enjoyed military success and prosperity, expanding its borders in every direction. With his kingdom established, David desired to build a permanent temple for the Lord. The Lord, however, told David that his record of bloodshed disqualified him from such holy work. Nonetheless, God promised David that his humility and zeal for God would be rewarded: God would establish David's dynasty perpetually, so that there would never cease to be a descendant of David reigning over Israel (2 Samuel 7).

After David's death, Israel continued to experience prosperity under the rule of his son Solomon. Solomon enhanced the prestige of the kingdom through numerous building projects, including the construction of a glorious Temple for the Lord in Jerusalem, Israel's capital. But Solomon's projects taxed the resources and patience of his subjects. In 922 BC, under Solomon's successor, the nation erupted in civil war. The Israelites divided into two kingdoms: Judah in the south (with its capital at Jerusalem), and Israel in the north (with its capital finally settling at Samaria). These two kingdoms continued to co-exist for two hundred years, sometimes as bitter enemies, and sometimes as allies. In Judah, the descendants of King David continued to reign. In Israel, however, several short-lived dynasties paraded across the scene, as no ruler seemed to be able to establish an enduring line of successors.

These numbers seem difficult to reconcile with the genealogy of Moses found in Exod 6:14–25, which places Moses only four generations from the entrance of Israel into Egypt. Also, Exod 1:11 and 12:37 state that the Israelites built the city of Ramesses, most likely a reference to Piramesse, which was expanded by Ramesses II (ca. 1279–1213 BC) and re-named in his honor. The Israelites could not have been building this city if they had left Egypt almost two centuries earlier. For a good overview of the issue, see Walton, "Exodus, Date of," 258–72.

In both kingdoms, God raised up prophets to warn the people to repent of their sins and resist the lure of pagan gods. But it was to no avail: as wickedness persisted, God was forced to judge the nations. First, the axe fell on Israel. In 721 BC, the Assyrians destroyed the northern kingdom, sending its people into exile in various regions around the empire. In their place, the Assyrians brought in people from neighboring countries so that the land would not go to waste (2 Kings 17). These people became known as Samaritans.

Judah did not suffer quite the same fate. After narrowly escaping the Assyrians, Judah seemed to enjoy a religious and political revival under the leadership of King Josiah (640–609 BC). But the revival was short lived: Josiah was killed in battle, and Egypt took control of Judah, placing Josiah's son Eliakim (renamed Jehoiakim) on the throne. The Egyptians were soon driven from Palestine by the Babylonians, and in 601 BC, Judah became subject to King Nebuchadnezzar of Babylon. But in 597 BC, Judah rebelled against its overlords, resulting in the deportation of many of its leading citizens. Then in 587 BC, Judah's last king, Zedekiah, again revolted against Nebuchadnezzar. This time, the king of Babylon was not inclined to mercy. Nebuchadnezzar laid siege to Jerusalem, and once its walls were breached, his wrath was fierce. King Zedekiah and his children were put to death. Jerusalem was destroyed, and its glorious temple reduced to ruin. Many of the people of Jerusalem were taken away to Babylon in what became known as the Babylonian Exile (2 Kings 23-25).

As the prophets had foretold, this exile was not very long-lived. In 538 BC, Babylon was conquered by Cyrus the Great and the Persian Empire. Cyrus issued a decree allowing all the captives to return to their homelands. Under the leadership of their governor Zerubbabel, several thousand of the Jewish people returned to rebuild Jerusalem, but many more chose to remain in Babylon, or even immigrate to Persia. In 515 BC, the Jewish people completed the reconstruction of their sacred sanctuary, initiating an era known as the Second Temple period. Led by their high priests, or sometimes under the direction of specially appointed governors like Ezra and Nehemiah, they slowly began the reconstruction of Judean society.

THE BEGINNING OF THE INTERTESTAMENTAL PERIOD[2]

The historical narratives of the Old Testament end with the stories of Ezra and Nehemiah. The story of God's people, however, was about to develop in some dramatic new directions. The Persian Empire was very different from those that had come before. It was well organized, with an efficient hierarchical chain of command that kept the imperial capitals thoroughly informed of the affairs in the provinces. The Jews seemed to have prospered under this system. Financial records from this period reveal that Jewish businessmen in Judea and other regions managed a great deal of wealth and commanded respect. Local affairs were generally run by the high priest, whose position became very prominent in this era. He was responsible for collecting the taxes that were paid to the regional governors known as "satraps." As long as these taxes were paid, the Jews were pretty much left to manage their own affairs, regulating their lives according to the "laws of the ancestors."

But the nation was hardly autonomous. It was subject to a foreign power, constrained by the will of the Gentile kings. Judea was free from Babylon, but still not free. There may have been efforts from time to time to revolt against Persia. We know such rebellions occurred among other vassals, but evidence of Judean participation is lacking. It is possible that the Jews, dispersed as they were throughout the Empire, lacked the will at this time to unite in an effort to reconstruct a free Judean state. Their pride broken and their situation not intolerable, they might have found it better to simply accept their lot and make the best of it. God would liberate Judah when and if it pleased him to do so.

In fact, the liberation from Persia took over two hundred years, and it did not come in the form that the Jews had anticipated. No Jewish prince would bring Persia to its knees. The conqueror would come from the West—and Judea would trade one foreign overlord for a rather more dangerous one.

THE GREEKS AND PERSIANS

The clash between the Persians and the Greeks had been brewing since the beginnings of the Persian Empire. It began in Asia Minor (modern

---

2. Most of our information about the history of intertestamental Judaism comes from the apocryphal books of 1 and 2 Maccabees and the writings of Josephus. The period of Greek rule in Judea is chronicled in Josephus Antiquities Books 12–13.

Turkey), where the Greeks had established several colonies. These colonies had been added to the Persian Empire by Cyrus the Great, but they were not willing subjects. In 499 BC, with the aid of the Greek city-state Athens, the colonies revolted. (At this time, Greece was not a united nation, but a land of several rival city-states.) The revolt was suppressed, but not before the Athenians had destroyed the city of Sardis, a loyal subject of Persia. That was all the excuse the Persians needed to declare war on the Athenians themselves. In 490 BC, Darius I landed his army on the Greek mainland, but the Athenians managed to repel them. In 481 BC, Darius' son Xerxes I invaded with an even larger army. Several of the Greek city-states laid aside their differences and formed a temporary alliance for the purpose of driving the eastern "barbarians" from their land. The Persians had to withdraw, but not before they had inflicted substantial damage on Athens. The Greeks were not inclined to forgive such indignities. But with the crisis passed, Athens, Sparta, and the other states resumed their old rivalries, and the invasion went unavenged.

But in 338 BC, Philip the Great, king of Macedonia, conquered and united all the Greek states under his leadership. Since the Greeks did not really consider the northern realm of Macedonia to be part of Greece, Philip had a difficult time persuading his subjects to cooperate. So to develop a sense of unity among the Greeks, he tried to turn their hatred away from one another and direct it toward a more useful target: the Persians. Philip began amassing a huge army and arousing Greek passions for a campaign against the eastern enemy. But he did not live to carry out his plan. He was assassinated in 336 BC, and his nineteen year old son Alexander became king in his place.

Alexander had to deal immediately with rebellious Greek states trying to test his mettle, but he proved more than equal to the task. He then wasted little time in carrying out his father's plan for Persia. In 334 BC, he crossed into Asia with an army of 40,000 men. His goal was rather modest: he was intent on the liberation of the Greek colonies in Asia Minor. But the incompetent Persian emperor Darius III, ignoring the threat posed by the ambitious Macedonian monarch, had left the western provinces of his empire almost totally without garrisons. Alexander easily overcame the little resistance he met, and achieved his initial goals quickly. And so, he decided to raise his sights from the liberation of a few colonies to the conquest of the Persian Empire. Thanks in part to his own charisma and brilliance, in part to the experience and training of his troops, and in part to the native peoples' unwillingness to sacrifice their lives for an unpopular overlord, Alexander accomplished the "liberation" of the Persian Empire's subjects in two years.

Alexander the Great did not live long to enjoy his conquests. He died suddenly in 323 BC, a mere thirty two years old. His young son, who had been left in the care of one of his generals until he came of age, was assassinated. Alexander's commanders then began to struggle among themselves to see who could take up the conqueror's mantle. As it turned out, none of them proved up to the task. Within a generation, Alexander's empire was carved into several rival kingdoms. Only two of the commanders—Ptolemy, who ruled Egypt and Palestine, and Seleucus, who took Babylon and Syria—managed to establish relatively stable dynasties. These Greek kings are known as the Diadochi, the Greek word meaning "successors."

THE JEWS UNDER GREEK RULE

With the coming of the Greeks, life changed dramatically for the Jewish people. The Persians had been rather unobtrusive in their rule, allowing the people of Judah to largely manage their own affairs. While the Jews who lived in Persia or traveled there frequently naturally adopted some of the language and customs of their overlords, they were not especially compelled to do so. So except for the burdens of taxation and conscription, the Jewish people remained essentially autonomous. But the Greeks had a very different style of leadership. Alexander the Great had been fully convinced the superiority of Greek culture, but his travels throughout the Persian provinces led him to believe that a merging of East and West would be the ideal. He symbolized the merger by holding a mass wedding in the Persian capital of Susa, presided over by Persian and Greek priests, in which Macedonian officers married noblewomen of Persia. After Alexander's death, most of his successors demonstrated their contempt for Alexander's vision by promptly divorcing their native wives. It was their intention to enjoy the victors' spoils, not to engage in social experimentation.

A new form of Greek-based culture known as "Hellenism" was taking root in the East. A vulgar form of the Greek language (known as Koine, meaning "common") became the official tongue of government and commerce. Any natives who wanted to curry the favor of the overlords learned to look and talk like a Greek, and they adopted Greek names, to complete the image. People from Greece and Macedonia began to immigrate to the East, believing it to be a good place to seek their fortune. Entire cities, like Antioch in Syria (capital of the Seleucid Empire), were established for these new residents. They served as enclaves of Greek civilization in the foreign Near Eastern environment. In other cities, Greeks and native peoples freely intermingled. Alexandria in Egypt was such a city. In these places, the close interactions could sometimes lead to trouble. In AD 38, a Greek had set up a pagan altar across the street from a Jewish synagogue in Alexandria, obviously for the purpose of antagonizing the Jews. It worked. Jewish residents tore down the altar in the night, resulting in a series of riots and persecution for the Jewish residents of the city.

After several years of struggles between the Diadochi, Judea fell into the hands of Ptolemy I, ruler of Egypt. From the Jewish viewpoint, this development must have appeared most baleful, indeed. Ptolemy held his native subjects in almost total contempt. Under his regime, native Egyptians were not allowed to hold positions of authority in the government or even to serve in the military, except in menial roles like cooks or water-bearers. They were taxed at higher rates than Greeks or Macedonians who settled in the land. Crops grown in Egypt were sold all over the Mediterranean, while Egyptian peasants went hungry. Ptolemy's attitude toward his subjects was so utterly exploitative that it has been said that he viewed Egypt simply as a money-making machine.

The people of Judea were not as directly affected by these policies as were the native Egyptians. Living at the extreme northern frontier, they were generally ignored by the empire, so long as they paid their taxes. Undoubtedly, however, those taxes were onerous. The Ptolemies believed that their right as conqueror was to punish their subjects—even if those subjects had not directly resisted the conquest! And so, the Jewish people felt their purses grow ever thinner, while the king in Egypt grew ever fatter. Their resentment must have been intense. Still, they were free to worship as they desired, and to live according to their ancestral customs. The governor of Judea, who at this time was the Jewish high priest, was allowed to administer his province with minimal interference. The spirit of Hellenism encouraged tolerance for the beliefs of others, even when the Greek found those beliefs repugnant.

But the situation was about to get worse. Much worse.

THE JEWS AND THE SELEUCIDS

In 200 BC, Antiochus III, king of the Seleucid Empire, managed to wrestle Palestine from Ptolemaic control. No doubt some of the Jews actually conspired with Antiochus to overthrow Egyptian rule, believing his regime would bring some improvement to their social and economic situation. Unlike the Ptolemies, the Seleucid regime had a reputation for a benevolent, almost paternal attitude toward their subjects. Also, since its capital was located in nearby Syria, many in Jerusalem probably thought they would be able to get more personal attention from the king than they had known under the Ptolemies. But hopes for a better future would soon be dashed. Antiochus had allied himself with another Greek king to quell the expansion of an upstart nation called "Rome." But Rome was tougher than it appeared, and dealt the Greek alliance a resounding defeat. Rome allowed the Seleucid Empire to remain in control of its Asian provinces, since the Romans had no interest yet in expansion into the area. However, Rome was very interested in money, and it forced the Seleucids to pay a lavish tribute to the conquerors. Antiochus was desperately in need of funds, and he determined to exploit the principal source at his disposal: his subjects. The people of Judea found themselves suffering under a tax burden even greater than they had known under the Ptolemies.

But that was only the beginning of sorrows. In Judea, there was a faction that believed it had a solution to the taxation issue, and perhaps a way of raising the Jews' esteem in the eyes of their overlords. In Seleucid policy, any native city that would reorganize itself as a Greek polis (city), complete with Greek-style senate, schools, and gymnasia—centers of physical training and athletic games honoring pagan gods—would be exempted from taxation. There was a small but influential segment of Judean society (the so-called "Hellenizers") that believed that Jerusalem should seek to be transformed into polis. They were probably outnumbered by those who preferred the traditional ways, but the Hellenizing faction had money, and money could buy power. In 174 BC, the Hellenizers approached Antiochus III's successor, his son Antiochus IV Epiphanes, with an offer he could not refuse: they would give him a great deal of money and raise even more tax revenue, if he would agree to depose the current high priest Onias and replace him with his more pro-Greek brother, Jason. Epiphanes accepted the deal enthusiastically.

The exchange established a very bad precedent. Soon, an even more radical faction came to Epiphanes with an even bigger bribe, and Jason was replaced with a man named Menelaus. While Menelaus was apparently a member of the priestly caste, he had no connection to the hereditary high priestly line, the family of Zadok, from whom the high priests had come since the days of King Solomon. But Menelaus needed no special qualifications for the work he seemed most interested in pursuing, which was lining his own pockets by plundering the Temple treasures. Extremely unpopular with the people, he faced resistance from both the traditionalists and the partisans of the deposed Jason.

When the throne of Egypt fell to a child in 168 BC, Antiochus Epiphanes believed his chance to conquer his great southern rival had arrived. He set out with his armies in order to overwhelm Egypt—but again, his plans were frustrated. Before Epiphanes had reached the northern Egyptian city of Alexandria, he was confronted not by the Egyptians, but by a Roman army. The Romans had no desire to see the Seleucid Empire conquer Egypt and take control of a major source of revenue and food for the Mediterranean region. So the Roman general demanded that Epiphanes leave Egypt immediately, not even granting the arrogant king time to formulate a way to retreat with his dignity intact. Well aware of Rome's might, Epiphanes had no choice but to comply. News of his humiliation spread quickly, and the story grew with the telling. By the time the rumor reached Jerusalem, it was being reported that Antiochus Epiphanes had been killed in battle. Jerusalem erupted in violence, and Jason's men forced Menelaus to retreat into the Temple complex (one of the most well fortified structures in Judea). Menelaus was under siege, but he somehow managed to send word to Antiochus Epiphanes that Judea was in revolt.

Epiphanes was outraged. First he had he been insulted by the Romans; now, the insignificant Judeans were challenging his authority! He set forth for Jerusalem, determined to make its people pay for their insubordination. Not only did he restore Menelaus to his position; he also decided that the Jewish religion itself needed to be reformed. Perhaps thinking he was doing the Jewish people a favor (since the "progressive" faction had asked permission to introduce more Greek culture in Jerusalem), Antiochus outlawed the distinctive Jewish practices of circumcision, keeping kosher, and Sabbath observance. Owning a copy of the Torah (Books of Moses) was made a capital offense. And the worst indignity of all: Antiochus had an altar devoted to the Greek god Zeus Ouranous ("God of the Heavens") set up in the Jerusalem temple.

The Jews would not be separated from their religion without a fight. Some sacrificed their lives, in the hope that their blood would provoke God's vengeance against the oppressors. Others took up arms to defend their faith. A group known as the Hasidim ("Pious Ones") became renowned for their valiant struggles against the Greeks, while maintaining such fidelity to the Law that they even chose to die rather than take up arms and defend themselves on the Sabbath day. But soon, a family known as the Hasmoneans emerged as the leaders of the resistance.[3] The patriarch of this clan, Mattathias Hashmon (Greek "Hasmoneus"), was a priest who resided in the city of Modein, near Jerusalem. When Greek officers arrived in his town and demanded he lead his people in a sacrifice to the pagan gods, the old priest killed the Greeks and fled with his sons into the wilderness. Mattathias did not lead this resistance movement for long, for he soon passed away, leaving the leadership of the rebellion to his oldest son, Judas (Greek form of "Judah") Hasmon. Judas was nicknamed "Maccabee," from an Aramaic word meaning "Hammer." This nickname became attached to the books that chronicle the rebellion, and thus the movement has somewhat mistakenly become known as the Maccabean Revolt. For three years the Hasmoneans and their allies waged a see-saw war against Antiochus' forces. Then in 164 BC, the Hasmoneans won a great victory, recapturing the Temple and removing the pagan altar. The eight-day ceremony of purifying and re-dedicating the Temple is still commemorated to this day in the feast of Hanukkah ("Dedication").

THE HASMONEAN PRIESTHOOD

Capturing the Temple was a great victory, but an even greater one was on the way: Antiochus Epiphanes was killed in battle against the Seleucid Empires' northern rivals, the Parthians. His successor, Antiochus V, had little interest in waging war on two fronts and continuing the oppression of the Jews. And so, by 163 B. C., the Jews' rights to worship as they pleased were restored. The persecution had ended.

---

3. The name "Hasmonean" is found only in the writings of Josephus; elsewhere, they are known as the Maccabees.

Most of the Jews, including the Hasidim, were happy to accept the offer of peace. But for Judas and his allies, the struggle was only beginning. The real enemy, in their eyes, was not the Seleucids, but the Hellenizing Jews. A tug-of-war began for the control of the Temple and the hearts of the Jewish people. Judas and his companions waged guerilla warfare against the Jerusalem establishment, winning some strategic victories and native support. But the Seleucids were not going to abandon their pro-Greek Judean allies. Around 161 BC, they sent a massive army into Judea to crush the Hasmonean forces. Judas met his end in the ensuing battle, but his younger brother Jonathan immediately stepped up as leader of the rebels. Jonathan led the faction for the next nineteen years, slowly building their strength and respectability.

During this time, the Seleucid Empire began having internal problems of its own, as various factions arose to compete for rule of the kingdom. These struggles frequently plunged the great realm into civil war. The Hasmoneans profited from these squabbles, taking advantage of the distraction to seize territory and fortify their position. They also found that they could exploit the situation by pitting rival claimants to the Seleucid throne against one another. In 153 BC, a pretender named Alexander Balas made Jonathan a most tempting offer: if he would help Balas overthrow the reigning Seleucid king Demetrius I, Balas would make Jonathan the high priest of Jerusalem and leader of Judea. Jonathan gladly accepted the offer. In 153 or 152 BC, he began his tenure by presiding over the observance of the Feast of Tabernacles. This development must have presented a dilemma to the traditionalists. On the one hand, Jonathan was a hero and a defender of the orthodox faith. On the other hand, he was no more from the traditional Zadokite high-priestly line than Menelaus had been.

Jonathan continued as high priest for the next ten years, and even managed to negotiate more honors from the Seleucids. After Balas had secured the throne, Jonathan was named the chief military commander and administrative officer of Judea. In 145 BC, Balas faced a new challenge from a man called Demetrius II, who claimed to be the son of Demetrius I and rightful heir to the throne. After Jonathan defeated one of Demetrius's general in battle, he was named "Kinsman of the King," one of the highest honors the king could bestow. But these rivalries would eventually prove his undoing. In 142 BC, he was enlisted to aid Balas's son, Alexander VI, to secure succession to the throne. As soon as

Jonathan had helped the new claimant take control of a portion of the kingdom, Alexander treacherously betrayed and murdered him.

Upon Jonathan's death, the youngest of the Hasmonean brothers, Simon, took over as high priest and leader of Judea. Since Judea was still part of the Seleucid Empire, he needed the official backing of a Syrian monarch for his administration to be considered legitimate. He was forced to turn to Demetrius II. But Simon knew that Demetrius II needed him as well, to provide mercenaries and safe passage for troops and supplies through his land. The two aspiring rulers worked out a deal: in exchange for military and tactical aid, Simon would be confirmed as spiritual and political leader of the Jews. Furthermore, Judea would be free from taxation, from foreign domination, and from Greek garrisons in the city. Judea would be practically, if not officially, emancipated from Greek rule. In 1 Macc13:41, the ratification of this treaty is commemorated as the time when Judea was freed from "the yoke of the Gentiles." (In actuality, it would be several years before Judea would be completely independent.) Simon's skills as a negotiator seemed to have pleased the Jewish people greatly. In 140 BC, an assembly was convened in Jerusalem, and Simon was acknowledged by the people as high priest and supreme military commander. Furthermore, they proclaimed that the position would become hereditary. The Hasmoneans had displaced the traditional Zadokite line as the family of the high priesthood.

Simon enjoyed several years of success and prosperity before he was assassinated by his own ambitious son-in-law, a man named Ptolemy, in 135 BC. Simon's son, John Hyrcanus, was acknowledged as high priest by the people of Jerusalem, but his tenure got off to a rocky start. While Ptolemy did not manage to take control of Judea, he was able kill Hyrcanus's mother and escape from justice. Then, an aggressive new Syrian monarch, Antiochus VII, took control of the Seleucid Empire. This competent and powerful king had no intention of allowing Judea to slip away from Greek control, given its strategic importance as a buffer between the Seleucids and the Ptolemies. Late in 135 BC, he invaded Judea, demolished several towns, and laid siege to Jerusalem itself. He demanded severe terms for its deliverance: a heavy tribute, a garrison of troops in Jerusalem, and—most humiliating of all—the destruction of Jerusalem's wall. Hyrcanus really had no choice but to comply.

Soon, however, Hyrcanus's fortune would change. Antiochus VII was killed in battle in 129 BC, and the Seleucid Empire was once again torn between rival claimants for the throne. Hyrcanus took advantage of this weakness to secure and expand his own nation. His conquests took him north to Samaria, where he destroyed the city of Shechem and the Samaritan temple on Mount Gerizim. This move was especially harsh: the Samaritans considered Mount Gerizim to be as holy as the Jews considered Mount Zion. This act of sacrilege further soured the already rocky relations between the Jews and Samaritans. To the south, Hyrcanus turned his attention to the Idumeans, descendants of the biblical Edomites. As he conquered several Idumean cities, he gave the inhabitants a choice: they could go into exile, or they could convert to Judaism. This policy of forced conversion would have serious future repercussions. For though the Idumean converts probably tried in good faith to follow the ways of Judaism, the Jews long considered them "half Jews," and treated them with contempt.

Hyrcanus expanded his territory with further conquests, adding several cities loyal to the Seleucids to his realm. In 111 BC, he conquered the city of Samaria (at that time, populated mainly by Greeks) and razed it to the ground. By the end of his reign, his kingdom was perhaps as large as that ruled by Solomon. He was acting in total independence of the Seleucids, paying no taxes, minting his own coins and making his own treaties. He did not, however, take the title "king," perhaps from deference to the biblical tradition that only descendants of David would rule in Judah. He also formed a significant "internal" alliance: according to Josephus, Hyrcanus felt he had been insulted by leaders of the Pharisee sect of Judaism, and so turned his attention and favor to their rivals, the Sadducees.

A FREE JEWISH STATE

John Hyrcanus died in 104 BC, the first Hasmonean to go to his grave peacefully. He had decreed that his widow would become ruler of the country after him, while his son Aristobulus I would take over the high priesthood. Aristobulus, however, had other plans. He ordered his mother imprisoned, and allowed her to starve to death in captivity. His brothers, too, were imprisoned as possible rivals. Only one brother, Aristobulus's close friend Antigonus, was allowed to remain free. This brother, however, soon fell victim to court intrigues, as Aristobulus was tricked by some unscrupulous advisors into having Antigonus executed. Overcome with grief at the loss of his only friend, Aristobulus became ill and died. His tenure had lasted less than a year, but it left an indelible mark on the Hasmonean dynasty. Like his predecessors, he continued to expand the Judean realm, forcing conquered people to convert to the Jewish religion. Among the new possessions was Galilee, the land where Jesus would live and minister. But these conquests are overshadowed by the darker aspects of his reign. Not only did Aristobulus set an unhealthy precedent of brutality, he also flouted tradition by claiming the title "king."

Aristobulus was succeeded in 103 BC by his brother Alexander Janneus. This monarch's long reign surely represents the darkest days of the Hasmonean kingdom. Like his predecessors, he added several new conquests to Judea, but these conquests did little to redeem his reputation in the eyes of posterity. He was generally rumored to be a scoundrel and a drunkard, and the people of Jerusalem so despised him that they once pelted him with lemons as he presided over religious observances for the Feast of Tabernacles. Early in his reign, he almost brought Judea to ruin when he attempted to double-cross Ptolemy Lathyrus, an aspirant to the throne of Egypt. Only the intervention of Cleopatra III, then queen of Egypt, delivered Judea from Ptolemy's rampaging army. Later in his reign, after he had suffered a crippling defeat at the hands of a rising Arabic nation called Nabatea, a group of Pharisees conspired with one of the Seleucid princes to remove Janneus from office. The people of Jerusalem came to Janneus's defense, however, and Janneus was delivered from the plot. He punished the conspirators by crucifying 800 of them in the center of Jerusalem.

Janneus died in 76 BC of an alcohol-induced illness. In a remarkable turn of events, he was succeeded to the throne by his widow, Salome Alexandra. (No doubt the energetic leadership of the Cleopatras in Egypt paved the way for such a move.) Since she could not serve as high priest, her eldest son, Hyrcanus II, took over this position. Her younger son, Artistobulus II, was given command of the armies. Salome proved a capable ruler, and generally won the support of the people. She broke with the policies of the preceding Hasmoneans by allying herself with the popular Pharisee party, rather than the more aristocratic Sadducees. She also broke with tradition by keeping clear of immorality or scandal. Her reign was marked by no great military victories or new alliances, but the country did not lose territory, either.

When Salome lay on her deathbed in 67 BC, she named her elder son Hyrcanus as her successor. Aristobulus, however, had other plans. He invaded Jerusalem and forced the high priest to take refuge in the Akra, a fortress in the center of the city. There Hyrcanus could have held out for a long siege, but instead, he offered to surrender. He agreed to allow Aristobulus to be both king and high priest, as long as Hyrcanus could retire in peace and continue to be supported in a manner fitting to his station. Aristobulus agreed to the terms, and Hyrcanus was free to settle down in Idumea on a fat government pension. Jerusalem breathed a sigh of relief, having avoided what could have been a bloody conflict.

But the negotiated peace was not long lived. There were several parties that preferred Hyrcanus over his brother: there were the people who had loved Alexandra and did not wish to see her will contravened; there were the Pharisees, who found Hyrcanus more favorable to their sect than Aristobulus; and most significant of all, there was the native governor of Idumea, a wily politician named Anitipater. Antipater believed that Hyrcanus would be more easily manipulated than his ambitious brother. These parties persuaded Hyrcanus that his life was in danger, since Aristobulus would not allow a potential rival to his throne to live. Antipater and Hyrcanus negotiated a deal with the king of Nabatea, Aretas III, and Aretas provided them with an army to put Hyrcanus back on the Judean throne. Soon Hyrcanus and the Nabatean troops arrived in Jerusalem, and Aristobulus found himself besieged in the Temple complex. His brief reign, it seemed, would soon be over.

THE ADVENT OF THE ROMANS[4]

In Syria, however, a situation was brewing that would have a profound effect on the Jews. The Roman general Pompey, one of the most powerful men in the world, had traveled to the east with his legions in order to deal with the ambitious Armenian king Tigranes. Tigranes had managed to conquer Mesopotamia, parts of Parthia, and even the remnants of the Seleucid Empire. He had easily dispatched the first Roman general he had met, and so Rome had decided it needed to take serious action against this threat to its eastern interests. One of Pompey's lieutenants, Aemilius Scaurus, had been stationed in Syria, while Pompey himself

---

4. The early era of Roman domination is recounted in Book 14 of Josephus's *Antiquities*.

went on to Armenia. Aristobulus and Hyrcanus wasted no time sending their emissaries to court Roman favor. Each offered a large bribe if Rome would agree to help their side secure control of Judea. Scaurus listened to both parties, and decided that Aristobulus was more likely to actually pay the bribe. Hyrcanus was ordered to lift his siege and withdraw his forces. Aristobulus was free, and for the time being, he was ruler of Judea once again.

After Pompey had finished with Tigranes (he generously allowed him to remain in power, but not-so-generously imposed a substantial tribute on his country), he went on to Antioch in Syria. There, he was met by three delegations from Judea: one representing Hyrcanus, one representing Aristobulus, and one claiming to represent the greater will of the Jewish people. This group asked for both the Hasmoneans to be deposed, a new high priest selected, and for Judea to be incorporated into the Roman Republic as a province. Pompey was on his way to deal with the Nabateans, and he did not wish to be detained. He ordered the brothers to keep the peace until he returned, when he promised to settle the squabble. But Aristobulus, fearing the decision would go against him, hastened to Jerusalem to fortify the city against the Romans.

Pompey was enraged by such insubordination. He postponed his trip to Nabatea and set out instead for Jerusalem. The Jewish residents welcomed him with open arms. But not Aristobulus—he had taken refuge in the Temple complex, the most formidable structure in the city. For three months Pompey laid siege to the Temple, until finally, on the Day of Atonement in 63 BC, his battering rams breached the gates. Giving full vent to their frustration, the Roman troops slaughtered the priests at the altars where they were performing their sacrifices. Aristobulus was captured alive and taken to Rome as a prisoner—along with many other residents of Jerusalem. Hyrcanus was installed as high priest of the Jews, but he was stripped of the title "king." Henceforth, Judea would be a subject to the Romans. The celebrated Jewish independence had come to an end.

THE HIGH PRIESTHOOD OF HYRCANUS II

As part of the Roman province of Syria, Judea was deprived of much of the prestige it had enjoyed when the Seleucids were in power. Hyrcanus II was the chief civil and religious authority in Judea, with the Idumean politician Anitpater acting as his chief advisor. But the Jewish state was under the direct authority of the Roman governor of Syria—from 65 BC to 62 BC, Aemilius Scaurus, the general who had first met the Jewish envoys in Syria. Under his administration, the Jerusalem authorities were still allowed to handle most matters of state themselves. Generally, the Roman overlords were unobtrusive, and Roman soldiers would have seldom been seen in Jerusalem. But nonetheless, Judea was in turmoil. The Romans liberated many of the Gentile territories captured by the Hasmoneans and returned them to their original owners. Jerusalem swelled with Jewish refugees who had been forced to abandon their homes. There were new taxes levied to pay the tribute demanded of all Roman possessions. And in spite of their general autonomy, the Jewish authorities could still be overruled by the Roman governors. The "yoke of the Gentiles" had returned.

But despite the upheavals, the situation in Judea was not completely dire. The Romans brought some obvious benefits to their subjects: the construction of roads and public buildings, Roman soldiers to keep them free from bandits, and the practical elimination of piracy on the sea. Trade could pass more freely throughout the Mediterranean region than ever before. All in all, the Jews could have prospered as part of the Roman Republic. The Romans were sometimes insensitive to local customs and beliefs, but being a practical people, they usually did not deliberately seek to provoke their subjects. This may be why a delegation of Jews had asked Pompey to incorporate Judea into the Roman province. The potential peace and prosperity of life under Rome must have seemed preferable to the misery that some of the Hasmoneans had brought about.

But several matters prevented the Jews from realizing peace. A major problem was the fact that the Romans seemed incapable of keeping their prisoners behind bars. In 57 BC, Aristobulus's elder son, Alexander, escaped from Pompey's custody and made his way back to Judea. There, he mustered an army and seized control of several important fortresses. The high priest Hyrcanus, with few military forces at his disposal, did not even try to engage Alexander. Instead, he attempted to protect himself by rebuilding the ruined walls of Jerusalem. Reluctantly, the Roman governor of Syria, Gabinius, accepted the responsibility for squelching the uprising. He engaged Alexander's army near Jerusalem and routed the rebels. Alexander fled to Alexandrium, a fortress located north of Jericho, while his remaining troops held two other fortresses.

Surprisingly, Alexander's mother convinced Gabinius to let her son go free, in exchange for turning the fortresses over to the Romans intact. Hyrcanus, on the other hand, did not fare so well from the incident. Seeing how badly he had handled the crisis, Gabinius decided that the high priest was incompetent to administer Judea. He ordered Judea divided into five administrative districts, each governed by its own "Sanhedrin" (senate). Hyrcanus retained his position as high priest and his religious authority, including his role as administrator of the Temple. But his civil authority was now nearly non-existent. For the first time in many generations, the high priest was not the official leader of the Jewish nation.

Aristobulus II and his sons continued to cause trouble in Judea for several years. In 56 BC, Aristobulus and his son Antigonus escaped from prison and attempted to capture a Judean fortress. The Romans quickly recaptured them, but at his mother's request, Antigonus too was allowed to remain in Judea. Then in 55 BC, while Gabinius was attending to business in Egypt, Alexander again incited revolt against Hyrcanus. Thirty thousand men rallied around Alexander, and Hyrcanus was essentially powerless against them. Gabinius hastily returned to Judea. Ten thousand of the rebels were killed and the revolt crushed, but once again, Alexander escaped.

JULIUS CAESAR AND THE JEWS

In 49 BC, the Roman civil wars had begun, and Pompey struggled with Julius Caesar for control of the East. Judea was an important pawn in this game because it could serve as a platform for launching an invasion of Egypt or Syria. Pompey summoned Hyrcanus and Antipater to his aid. But Caesar, too, recognized the strategic importance of Judea. Seeking an ally who could rally the Jews against Hyrcanus and Pompey, he chose Aristobulus II, a man who had demonstrated his ability to gather a following. Caesar released him from prison and put two legions of soldiers at his command. But Aristobulus never made it to Jerusalem—he was poisoned to death by Pompey's men while still in Rome. A similar fate befell his son Alexander, who was arrested by one of Pompey's generals and beheaded. Only Antigonus escaped, fleeing to Egypt.

Hyrcanus and Antipater were soon freed of their obligations to Pompey, who was assassinated in Egypt in 48 BC. Julius Caesar had pursued Pompey to Egypt, but finding his rival already dead, he became embroiled in the dispute between King Ptolemy XIII and his older sister Cleopatra VII. Cleopatra had led the kingdom when their father had died, and she considered herself the true ruler of Egypt. But once Ptolemy had come of age, most Egyptians favored him as king, forcing Cleopatra into exile. Caesar had traveled to the palace in Alexandria planning to forge an alliance with Ptolemy, but Cleopatra intercepted him and seduced him into an alliance with her, instead. Caesar then turned on the Egyptian king and imprisoned him in the royal palace. One of Ptolemy's generals, however, rallied the Egyptian army and roused the Alexandrian citizens against the Roman general and the queen. Now it was Caesar and his men who were imprisoned. It was a golden opportunity for Hyrcanus and Antipater to ingratiate themselves to their new overlord. Hyrcanus persuaded the Jews of Egypt to side with Caesar, while Antipater brought an army of 3000 men to his aid. Soon, Roman troops arrived as well, and Caesar was liberated. King Ptolemy died attempting to escape from the palace, and Cleopatra became the undisputed ruler of Egypt.

Cleopatra journeyed to Rome with her lover, seeking to win over the people of the great city just as she had captivated their leader. But while the exotic lady fascinated the masses, she appalled the Senate. The conservative Romans abhorred the notion of a woman wielding political power, and were scandalized by Caesar and Cleopatra's flagrant adultery (while noble Romans usually had lovers, they tended to be discrete about it). But most of all, the senators feared that the queen of Egypt intended to rule Rome. It did not help matters when she and Caesar bore a son and named him Caesarion. Cleopatra was convinced that Caesarion would one day rule the world. The Senate, however, had ideas of its own.

While Caesar was making enemies in Rome, he had not forgotten his Jewish benefactors. Antipater was made a Roman citizen, a position of considerable privilege in those days. In addition, he was named "procurator" of Judea, essentially meaning that he was Rome's emissary among the Jews. Hyrcanus was made the "ethnarch"—chief governmental authority—of the Jews, restoring the civil authority that Gabinius had stripped from him. The Jews were also permitted to fortify Jerusalem, another right that Gabinius had taken from them. And perhaps most important of all, Caesar enacted legislation protecting the Jewish religion from persecution. Throughout the Roman realm, the Jews were free to practice the customs of their ancestors without interference.

THE RISE OF HEROD

Although Hyrcanus was officially the leader of Judea, the ambitious Idumean Antipater was conniving his way into even more power. He used his own considerable wealth, as well as pilfered public funds, to secure government positions for his two oldest sons. The eldest, Phasael, was appointed governor of Jerusalem and its environs, while the second son, Herod, became the governor of Galilee. Herod was a vigorous young man, at the age of twenty-five already displaying the drive that would one day make him king. One of his first acts as governor was to clean out the bandits in the Galilean countryside. Because these bandits usually preyed on rich merchants, they were often viewed by masses as the folk heroes. When Herod arrested and executed a bandit named Hezekiah, the action met praise from some Galileans and the Syrians. But the Jerusalem Sanhedrin argued that Herod had overstepped his authority, since only the Sanhedrin could try and execute criminals. Most likely, some Sanhedrin members saw the incident as an opportunity to curtail the growing power of Antipater and his sons. They summoned Herod to Jerusalem to stand trial.

He answered the Sanhedrin's summons. But instead of appearing before the ruling council dressed in mourning clothes, as was typical for a man accused of a serious crime, he came dressed in the purple robes of a ruler and surrounded by a retinue of armed men—ready to defend Herod, should the Sanhedrin attempt to take him into custody. When it looked as if the Sanhedrin was going to convict Herod of murder, the high priest Hyrcanus intervened and called for a recess. He took Herod aside and advised him to flee Jerusalem, before the trial could resume. Herod heeded the advice, and left Jerusalem to take refuge with the Roman governor Sextus. Through more bribery, Herod was confirmed in his position as governor, and given further authority as the strategos (military commander) of some native forces in Syria-Palestine. Now, with an army at his disposal, Herod marched into Jerusalem, intent on avenging his humiliation by the Sanhedrin. Only the pleas of his father Antipater prevented Herod from initiating a bloodbath. He returned to Galilee, confident that he had demonstrated that he was no one to trifle with.

Roman politics continued to wreak havoc on Judean affairs. In 44 BC, Julius Caesar was assassinated, and the long and difficult struggle for leadership of the Republic commenced. One of the assassins, Cassius, began to amass an army to fight against Caesar's lieutenant,

Mark Antony. The governor of Syria supported Cassius, and Hyrcanus and Antipater were obligated to follow suit. Cassius taxed the province heavily in order to supply his troops, selling whole towns into slavery if they failed to raise their tribute. But Antipater and his son Herod proved most helpful in persuading the Jewish towns to pay their taxes. Cassius was impressed by their abilities, and confirmed Herod in his position as strategos. When Antipater was assassinated in 43 BC, Herod lost an important mentor and ally. But by now, the young man was coming into his own. He easily repulsed an attempt by Antigonus, the remaining son of Aristobulus, to seize control of Judea. Even the people of Jerusalem were impressed with the action, and hailed Herod as a hero.

Meanwhile, Cassius and his ally Brutus had been defeated by Mark Antony and Octavian (who would later be called Augustus). The two conquerors, along with their partner Lepidus, divided the provinces between them: Octavian and Lepidus ruled in the West, while Antony took the East. Antony's army had been seriously depleted by the war, and he had many debts to pay. Seeking allies who would be useful in raising money and recruiting soldiers, he confirmed Herod and his brother Phasaelus in their positions, and conferred on each of them the title "tetrarch"—a position second in eminence only to that of ethnarch. Hyrcanus remained the ethnarch, and he continued as the high priest and figurehead leader of Judea. Antony further demonstrated his good will by emancipating the Jews whom Cassius had sold into slavery.

But Antony's real preoccupation at this time was Egypt and its queen. When Julius Caesar had been assassinated, Cleopatra had fled Rome, suspecting that her life and the life of her son Caesarion were in danger. Returning to Egypt, she had spent three years strengthening her faltering kingdom. Antony recognized Cleopatra as the second-greatest power in the East (after himself), and knew that she would be an important ally. Cleopatra, for her part, knew that she would need Roman help to rebuild her kingdom. So Antony and Cleopatra became allies and lovers—he, with hopes of a new source of revenue, and she with dreams of a second chance at world domination. Antony spent the winter of 41–40 BC in Alexandria in the company of the queen.

With Antony's army weak and his attention diverted, the Parthians (who had already proven themselves a match for the Romans) seized the moment and invaded Syria and Palestine. Antigonus immediately sought an alliance with the invaders. With bribes and promises of plunder, he hired some Parthian troops to help him take Jerusalem. But when their first attack was turned away, the determined Hasmonean tried a different tactic. Unable to get to his enemies within the city, he would lure them out, instead. Antigonus bribed a Parthian officer to invite Hyrcanus, Herod, and his brother Phasaelus to a meeting to discuss an alliance between Jews and Parthians. Herod suspected a trap and refused the invitation. Phasaelus and Hyrcanus, however, went to the Parthian camp, where they were soon taken captive. Phasaelus was killed, but Hyrcanus was spared for the time being: since Old Testament law forbids men with physical defects from serving as high priest, Antigonus merely cut off his uncle's ears, effectively eliminating the old man as a rival for the leadership of Judea.

As the Parthian troops descended on Jerusalem, Herod was forced to flee. Taking his wives, children, and a sizable company of men, he first battled his way to Idumea, gathering what resources he could muster. From there, he went east toward Arabia, hoping to get some aid from the Nabateans. But the king of Nabatea had no interest in coming into conflict with Parthia. Herod was on his own.

ANTIGONUS I

Antigonus began his reign in Judea in 40 BC. Like the Hasmoneans of old, he claimed both the high priesthood and the throne. The coins minted in his reign identify him by his Hebrew name, Mattathias—the same name borne by the father of the Hasmoneans, who had set the entire revolt in motion. It was an ironic epithet, since Antigonus would be the last of the Hasmonean priest-kings.

We know little of the internal affairs during Antigonus's reign. Josephus focuses instead on Herod, who would play such a major role in Judean politics. Herod recognized that without Roman support, he could not hope to recapture Jerusalem. As an Idumean, he would receive little sympathy from the native Jews. So after being rebuffed in Nabatea, Herod made his way first to Egypt, and then to Rome. Antony was there, and he was sympathetic to Herod's cause (and appreciative of Herod's bribes). Antony pleaded Herod's case before the Senate, and even requested that they name him king of Judea—an outcome better than Herod could have hoped for. The Senate approved the proposal. In less than seven days, Herod had gone from pitiful refugee to king of Judea.

But before he could claim the throne, he had to deal with Antigonus. The current Roman governor of Syria, Ventidius, had managed to expel the Parthians from the region, but as long as Antigonus paid his tribute (and no doubt some bribes, as well), Ventidius chose to ignore Rome's order to depose him. But when Herod arrived in Syria with a Roman army in 39 BC, he demanded Ventidius's cooperation, and finally received it. For the next two years, the battle went back and forth, as Herod was unable to secure decisive victory with Roman troops that were frequently called away to other duties. But finally, in 37 BC, Jerusalem was captured, and Antigonus was delivered to the Romans. He was taken to Antioch in Syria, where (at Herod's request) he was beheaded. It was the first time the Romans had ever carried out such a sentence on a king.

So ended the reign of the Hasmonean priest-king. The Jews remained vassals of Rome, subject to the whims of its generals and senate. But now, they were governed by a Roman client king, the crafty and capricious King Herod.

HEROD'S CONSOLIDATION OF HIS KINGDOM[5]

No doubt Herod the Great is most famous for the "Slaughter of the Innocents," his attempt to do away with the Christ child by killing all the baby boys of Bethlehem (Matt 2:16–18). But while his legacy has been one of incredible evil, it was not for naught that history conferred on Herod the title "the Great." He was an energetic and competent ruler who raised Judea's status in the Roman Empire and brought almost unprecedented splendor to Jerusalem. He was a complex, insecure, and tragic figure who longed for respect from subjects that generally despised him.

After taking the throne in 37 BC and for about a decade after, Herod's main task was securing his rule against any contenders for the throne. He proceeded by executing all of Antigonus's supporters, taking their property and using it to reward his benefactors. He also ransomed Hyrcanus from the Parthians, giving him a position of honor at public events. Josephus tells us that Herod's real intention was to bring Hyrcanus close enough to kill him. But publicly, Hyrcanus was treated as an honored patriarch. Herod also married Hyrcanus's daughter Mariamne. It seems like a political move on the surface, like David's marriage to Saul's

---

5. Josephus gives a rather detailed account of Herod's reign in Books 15–17 of his Antiquities.

daughter Michal—an effort to legitimize Herod's rule. But apparently, Herod was actually devoted to the woman. In fact, his jealousy for her would eventual lead to the downfall of the Hasmoneans.

Since he couldn't serve as the high priest, Herod installed an old friend named Hananel in the office. Hananel came from an undistinguished family, and since he had been living in Babylon, he had no political clout in Jerusalem at all. Herod hoped this appointment would prevent the high priest from becoming a potential source of competition. But Herod's shrewish mother-in-law, Alexandra—daughter of Hyrcanus, and mother of Herod's wife Mariamne—demanded that Herod install her son Aristobulus III, a sixteen-year-old youth, as high priest. She enlisted the aid of another ambitious mother, Queen Cleopatra, who persuaded Mark Antony to order Herod to install the young Hasmonean as high priest. Antony was probably unaware that he was signing the teen's death warrant.

Aristobulus III was a handsome youth and he won the hearts of the Jews. Such competition Herod would not tolerate. So one day while Aristobulus was swimming in a pool at his mother's house, Herod's servants "accidentally" drowned the young man. Hananel once again took over the high priesthood. Alexandra complained bitterly to Cleopatra, who insisted that Antony investigate the incident. (Cleopatra had hopes that Herod would be deposed, and Judea would be added to her kingdom.) But Herod knew how to deal with the Roman general: he approached Antony with bribes and promises of further support. Antony dismissed the charges. With Alexandra's ambitions stymied, she concentrated her efforts on inciting Mariamne's growing suspicion of her husband.

Alexandra was a constant annoyance to Herod, but Cleopatra was a more serious problem, being determined to add Judea to her Egyptian empire. Antony would not give her Herod's kingdom, since he considered the Idumean an important ally, but he did give her some valuable properties in Judea. Cleopatra further annoyed Herod by involving him in a conflict with Nabatea. The king of Nabatea was withholding his tribute, and Cleopatra persuaded Antony make Herod responsible for collecting the money, hoping the two kingdoms would weaken one another and become easy prey. The plan worked well for a while, with Herod and the Nabateans fighting a see-saw struggle that was crippling both sides. But when the Nabateans murdered some Judean envoys that had been sent to negotiate a truce, the outraged Jews rallied and routed the Nabateans. The tribute was restored, and Herod once again received the praise of his overlords.

Herod's problems with Cleopatra came to a dramatic end when Mark Antony was defeated by Octavian (Augustus) at the Battle of Actium in 31 BC. Herod would soon have a new master. But before meeting with Octavian, Herod wanted to make certain that there could be no rival claimants to the Judean throne. And so, he had Hyrcanus accused of conspiring with the Nabateans against Judea and Rome (a charge that was almost certainly false, since Hyrcanus had no ambition for such an undertaking). With the old priest convicted and executed, Herod felt his claim on the throne was more secure than ever. Herod also had Alexandra and Mariamne placed under guard in one of his fortresses, giving instructions that if he was sentenced to death, Mariamne should be executed as well. The king could not bear the thought of another man having Mariamne, even after his death. Unfortunately for them both, Mariamne found out about the order, and she began to loathe her unbalanced husband.

With all things set in order, Herod set out to meet Octavian. Presenting himself as the hapless victim of Antony and Cleopatra's treachery, he gained the new ruler's sympathy. Not only was he confirmed in his position as king of the Jews, he was granted other honors, as well. After Antony and Cleopatra had committed suicide, Octavian retuned to Herod the lands that Cleopatra had taken, along with Samaria and some important coastal cities. The king had weathered the storm quite well.

When he returned to Jerusalem, Herod found his wife cold and distant. The king was confused and heartbroken, probably imagining his success would have elevated him in her eyes. But others in the royal household, recognizing the tension between Herod and Mariamne, decided to exploit the animosity. Herod's mother Cyprus and his sister Salome, envious of the aristocratic Mariamne, began spreading rumors that she had been unfaithful during Herod's absence. Salome actually bribed the king's cupbearer to charge that Mariamne had tried to poison Herod. Herod's investigations uncovered that one of his officers had revealed to Mariamne that she was to be killed if Herod did not return from his meeting with Octavian. This meager evidence was enough for Herod to conclude that the rumors of adultery were true. Mariamne was tried and executed in 29 BC. Her mother Alexandra, justifiably angry, attempted to persuade some officers to join her in rebellion against

Herod. The plot was revealed, however, and in 28 BC, Alexandra, too, was executed. Thus all the threats to Herod's reign had been eliminated.

HEROD'S PRODUCTIVE YEARS

Herod was devastated by the loss of Mariamne, but after he recovered from his grief, he began the most productive phase of his reign. Under the rule of Octavian—who (in 27 BC) was proclaimed emperor, and given the title Augustus—the Roman Empire was enjoying a period of unprecedented peace and prosperity, and Judea was reaping the benefits. Herod traveled often to Rome, where he was well respected. His two sons by Mariamne, named Aristobulus and Alexander, were sent to Rome for schooling. Herod formed a friendship with Augustus's second-in-command, Vipsanius Agrippa, and even named one of his grandsons in Agrippa's honor (the King Herod Agrippa of Acts 12). These relationships paid dividends: several times, new lands were added to Herod's realm, so that at its greatest extent, it was at least as big as the Hasmonean kingdom. Augustus honored Herod by conferring on him the title *rex socius* ("allied king"), a position that granted Herod liberty far beyond that of most Roman "client kings." In all internal matters of state, Judea was basically free from Roman interference.

Herod worked hard to impress the Romans and the Gentiles living in his realm. He surrounded himself with Greek counselors, and gave his children a fine Greek education in Rome. He rebuilt several cities according to the model of the Greek poleis, and gave them Greek names. The ancient port city of Straton's Tower was renovated in Greek style, and re-named Caesarea. Equipped with a theater, hippodrome, and amphitheater, it became the foremost port of Asia, and a showplace for Greek culture and religion in the East. The city of Samaria, destroyed by John Hyrcanus, was also rebuilt, equipped with a temple for the royal cult, and re-named Sebaste (Greek for "Augustus"). In the Gentile cities of Herod's realm, he built or embellished many temples dedicated to Augustus Caesar and the Greek deities.

Herod was in a difficult position, trying to appear a sophisticated man of the world to outsiders, while trying to be a good and pious Jew in the eyes of his subjects. He generally avoided giving unnecessary offense to the Jews' religious scruples. His coins and buildings contained no portraits of himself or other human figures, since some Jews regarded any such images as a violation of the biblical commandment against graven images. His palaces all included immersion pools, so he and his company could observe the ritual purity that the Law prescribed (washing before meals, bathing after sexual relations or menstrual periods, etc.). He was careful to eat a kosher diet, even when he traveled abroad. He also worked as an advocate for Jews throughout the Empire, so that Jewish people everywhere could follow the commandments of God without hindrance.

But Herod's most elaborate attempt to win the admiration of his people (while assuring his own place in history) was his expansion of the Jerusalem Temple. He lavished his personal and public funds on the structure, expanding and beautifying it until it was a wonder of the ancient world. The priests and rabbis, suspicious of Herod's motives when he proposed the Temple renovation, required that Herod agree not to suspend worship during the construction, and not to allow any impious workmen to take part in the project. He fulfilled these obligations by having the new building constructed around the existing structure, while services continued uninterrupted. The construction was done by priests, specially trained in carpentry techniques. While much of the architecture copied the popular Greek styles of the day, Herod still avoided any human or animal imagery that might offend Jewish scruples. Even the rabbis, who had nothing good to say about Herod, remarked that no one could claim to have seen beauty unless they had seen Herod's Temple.

But in spite of these accomplishments, Herod was still despised by many of his subjects. Part of this enmity was simple prejudice, since Herod was Idumean by birth. But his domestic policies surely did nothing to endear him to his subjects. He was, in a word, a despot. He would endure no challenges to his authority. The Jerusalem senate, the Sanhedrin, was gutted of its civil power and allowed to judge religious matters only. Many of its members were massacred because they had supported Antigonus over Herod. He also deprived the high priesthood of its civil power, and prevented it from becoming a center for nationalistic ideals by filling the post with obscure individuals and foreigners. His last appointee was awarded the post simply because Herod had fallen in love with the man's daughter, and the king couldn't marry a mere commoner. His paranoia compelled him to ban public assembly or "seditious" speech, and to dispatch spies throughout his realm to report any suspicious behavior or talk. It also inspired many of his building projects, including a stronghold in Jerusalem, the fortress city of Herodium, and a renovation of the old fortress city Masada in the Judean wilderness. In the latter years of his reign, he often sequestered himself away in one fortress or another, hiding from potential assassins.

Of course, all this construction required money, and lots of it. Some of the funds Herod provided personally, but much more came from taxation. There were taxes collected directly from the Judean citizens that paid the tribute to Rome and funded public services. There were also taxes on the transportation of goods, and a "temple tax" that supported the Temple complex. But Herod also levied taxes on merchants traveling the trade routes that passed through his territories or who used his ports. These business taxes brought in a great deal of revenue. So while the natives might have chafed under the combination of tribute, taxes, and tithes, the average resident of Palestine probably did not find the burden too oppressive during Herod's reign.

HEROD'S FINAL YEARS

Herod's prosperity continued until about 13 BC. In fourteen years, he had made Judea a significant realm in the Roman Empire. His building projects were renowned. And the friendship he had forged with the Romans would continue to pay dividends to the Jewish people for centuries to come. But now, the family troubles that had been brewing for so long caught up with him, and his remaining years were miserable.

Herod's family life had always been a mess. He married ten times in all and fathered many children. His first wife was a commoner named Doris, who had borne him a son named Antipater. He divorced her and sent her away after he married Mariamne the Hasmonean. He loved Mariamne's two sons, Alexander and Aristobulus, but they were understandably resentful when Herod killed their mother. When they returned from Rome in 17 BC, the tension was thick, and Herod's jealous sister Salome exacerbated the situation. She told Herod that the young men were plotting to assassinate him and take his throne for themselves. Herod responded by recalling his first wife Doris and his son Antipater from their banishment, believing that Mariamne's sons wouldn't dare assassinate him when Antipater was officially first in line for the throne. Finally, in 7 BC, Salome, Antipater, and Herod's brother Pheroras fabricated evidence that Alexander and Aristobulus were plotting Herod's assassination. Herod ordered the young men strangled to death.

With the Hasmoneans out of the way, the older brother Antipater decided to seize the throne. If he had only remained patient a couple years, it would probably have come to him naturally, since Herod was about seventy years old and in failing health. But fearing that his father might actually outlive him or appoint one of his other half-brothers as heir, Antipater conspired with his uncle Pheroras to poison Herod's wine. Through a strange twist of fate, however, the tainted cup accidentally came to Pheroras, instead. Through torture, Herod discovered that the poison had been intended for him, and that it had come from Antipater. Antipater was arrested and beheaded.

It would have been during these last years of his life that Herod would have received the fateful visit from the Magi that prompted the Slaughter of the Innocents. Given how jealously Herod had protected his throne even from his own sons, it is not surprising that the news of the birth of a new "king" in Judea would have elicited such a violent reaction from him. Herod's paranoia had progressed to near insanity. He moved frequently from one of his fortresses to another, attempting to confuse any would-be assassins. He changed his will frequently as well, and kept its contents a closely guarded secret. In this manner, he hoped to discourage any of his sons from hastening his departure from the land of the living.

Through the last year of his life, Herod suffered from a degenerative condition that caused him constant physical agony. Josephus reports that he suffered agony in his bowels, a "putrefaction" of his privates, difficulty in breathing, and that a foul odor hung about him, making his presence unbearable. There has been much speculation as to the cause of this condition, including chronic kidney disease, gangrene, and scabies. To Josephus, it was a judgment of God. Even in his final days, Herod did not cease from his offensive behavior. As his death neared, he ordered that the patriarchs of all the noble families in Judea were to be taken captive, and that when Herod died, they were to be slain. In this manner, Herod planned to ensure that there would be great mourning at his death. Fortunately, this command was not carried out.

Most scholars agree that the death of Herod occurred in 4 BC. Josephus reports that Herod died after a lunar eclipse and shortly before Passover. There was a partial eclipse in 4 BC that occurred 29 days before Passover that year. Furthermore, Josephus states that Herod's son Philip died in the twentieth year of Tiberius Caesar (ca. AD 34) after a thirty-seven year administration, placing the beginning of his administration at around 4 BC. Nonetheless, the evidence is not conclusive, and other dates are sometimes advocated, including either 5 BC, in which there were two lunar eclipses, and 1 BC, in which there was one. Josephus tells us that Herod was buried at Herodium with all the pomp befitting a king. The location of the tomb itself, however, was lost for many centuries. It apparently has now been discovered by Israeli archeologists.[6]

HEROD'S SUCCESSORS[7]

At Herod's death, Judea erupted in violence, and his eldest remaining son, Archelaus, immediately had to put down riots in Jerusalem. He then traveled to Rome, where he was expecting to be confirmed as king of Judea (an episode alluded to by Jesus in Luke 19:12–26). But as soon as Archelaus had departed, trouble broke out anew. This time, Varus, the governor of Syria, brought in Roman soldiers to stop the fighting. When the Roman officer charged with keeping peace in Jerusalem attempted to plunder the Temple treasures, there was still more rioting. Nor was the trouble confined to Judea: in Galilee, a bandit named Judas ben Hezekiah plundered the royal arsenal in the city of Sepphoris and began pillaging throughout the region. In Perea, a man named Simon was declared king of the Jews. Varus had to bring in more Roman troops, and even called on help from the Nabateans to put down the insurrection breaking out throughout the land. The operation has become known as the "War of Varus."

Meanwhile, in Rome, Archelaus's claim to the throne was being disputed by his brother Antipas and other members of the royal house, who argued that Herod's final will was invalid. Eventually, however, Augustus decided to abide by the general provisions of Herod's final will, but with an important exception. Archelaus was declared ruler of Judea, but with the rank of ethnarch, not king. Another son named Philip was installed as the tetrarch (a regional governor) of Batanaea, Trachonitis, Auranitis, Gaulanitis, Panias, and other territories east of the Jordan. Antipas—who became known simply as Herod—became the tetrarch of Galilee.

Philip proved a capable ruler. His was a peaceful reign, unmarred by scandal or rebellion. Like his father, he was a builder. His most note-

---

6. Associated Press, "Archaeologists Find Tomb of King Herod."
7. See Josephus, Antiquities Books 17–18, and the shorter account in War Book 2.

worthy project was building a city at Paneas, which he named Caesarea. It came to be known as "Caesarea Philippi," to distinguish it from the important coastal city built by his father. His productive reign ended with his death in AD 33 or 34.

Herod Antipas was an ambitious and crafty leader, described as a "fox" by Jesus (Luke 13:32). He was apparently similar in temperament to his father, though he seems to have lacked his competence. Like Philip, he was a builder, constructing a fine city in Galilee called Tiberias, named after Augustus's successor. Unfortunately, the city had mistakenly been constructed over an old cemetery. Since the Jews considered human remains to be a source of ritual impurity, they refused to settle in, or even enter, Tiberias. Antipas had more luck with some of his other projects, refurbishing and fortifying Sepphoris in Galilee and Betharamphtha in Perea.

Like Herod the Great, Herod Antipas also had his share of family problems. In AD 14, he was married to the daughter of Aretas, the king of Nabatea. The wedding was probably inspired by politics rather than passion, since the emperor Augustus encouraged marriages among his vassals as a way of keeping peace in his kingdom. But while visiting his brother Philip, Antipas fell in love with Herodias, his brother's wife. Herodias shared his passion, and she was willing to divorce her husband to marry Antipas. Since polygamy was still acceptable in that day, Antipas could have taken Herodias as a second wife, but Herodias would not permit it. The proud aristocrat was unwilling to play "second fiddle" to the daughter of the Nabatean king. So in about AD 27, Antipas divorced the Nabatean princess and married the woman he truly loved. To King Aretas, however, the insult to his daughter was unforgiveable. He was already at odds with Antipas regarding a border dispute; this divorce was the last straw. Around AD 36, Aretas sent his army out against Antipas, who responded by dispatching his own troops. But Antipas's army was betrayed by some Jewish traitors, and taken by surprise, it was completely destroyed. Aretas was satisfied that his daughter's honor had been avenged.

Matthew 14 and Mark 6 report that Herod's marriage to Herodias led to the execution of John the Baptist. John had been critical of Herod's marriage to his half-brother's wife, saying it was "not lawful" for him to have her. While there were no Old Testament laws against marrying a divorced woman, there were several possible bases for John's objection.

First of all, many writers note that rabbinic interpretations of the Law forbid a man from marrying his brother's wife, except when the brother had died and left no male heir. Thus, it may not have been a written law that Herod Antipas had violated, but an oral interpretation of the law. Furthermore, John may have shared Jesus' belief that it is immoral for a man to divorce his wife for trivial reasons (see Matt 19:3–12). Finally, Herodias was Antipas's niece, and the Dead Sea Scrolls demonstrate that some Jews, at least, believed that the Law forbade a man from marrying his niece.[8] In any event, John's criticism did not sit well with Herod Antipas, and he had John arrested. After John had been imprisoned a while, the fateful incident occurred that brought about his death. Herod's step-daughter Salome had danced for the governor, pleasing him so that he made that oft-heard vow to give her whatever she asked, up to half his realm. At her mother's instigation, Salome requested the head of John the Baptist. Herod ordered John beheaded (Matt 14:1–12; Mark 6:14–29; Luke 9:7–9), probably around AD 28 or 29.

Josephus, however, gives a somewhat different account of the execution. He claims that Herod Antipas feared John would begin an insurrection, since the masses would do most anything John desired. Very likely both accounts hold some truth: John's criticism of Herod's personal life may have nettled Herod, but his official reason for arresting John was the danger of revolt. It would have been this rationale that Herod would have reported to his Roman overlords. In any event, Josephus reports that the Jewish people were outraged by John's execution. In AD 36, when Aretas attacked Galilee and decimated Antipas's army, many believed it was a divine judgment for Antipas's murder of John the Baptist.

Antipas met his comeuppance because of a conflict with his own nephew Agrippa, who was also brother of Herodias (this Agrippa is the "King Herod" of Acts 12). Agrippa, who was a wild, irresponsible lad, had run up extensive debts living the high life in Rome. Herodias persuaded Antipas to give money to her brother to keep him out of prison, but Antipas made no secret of his contempt for the young profligate. In AD 37, however, Agrippa's fortune changed when his good friend Caligula became the emperor of Rome. Caligula rewarded his erstwhile drinking buddy by making him king of the domain previously governed by the late brother Philip. When Herodias learned of her brother's good

---

8. This prohibition is found in 11Q19, the "Temple Scroll," and the fragmentary text designated 4Q251.

fortune, she urged her husband to ask Caligula to make him a king, as well. But Agrippa was still smarting from Antipas's superior attitude, and he sent Caligula documents that suggested that Antipas was conspiring with the Parthians against Rome. When he could not adequately refute the charges, Antipas was sentenced to exile in Gaul, where he died in AD 39. To her credit, when Herodias was given the choice of remaining in the comfort of her home or accompanying her husband into exile, she chose the latter.

Philip was loved, and Herod Antipas was tolerated. But Archelaus managed to alienate not only his subjects but his overlords, as well. The son of the Idumean Herod and a Samaritan mother, he had two strikes against him in Jewish eyes before he ever took office. Yet prejudice alone cannot account for the animosity he generated. Josephus gives us few details about his reign, but it must have been disastrous. In AD 6, when Augustus launched an investigation of Palestinian affairs, a joint Judean-Samaritan delegation traveled to Rome to present formal complaints against Archelaus. Considering the strained relationship between the Jews and Samaritans, only a thoroughly corrupt governor could have brought them together. Augustus believed their complaints, and he banished Archelaus to Gaul. Judea was taken from the hands of the Herodians and placed under the direct administration of a Roman governor, who was answerable to the regional governor in Syria.

THE ROMAN GOVERNORS OF JUDEA

In Jesus' day, the Judean governor was called a *"prefect,"* but later he was known by the title *"procurator."* Generally, only truly unruly provinces were directly administered by a Roman official, in locations where it was deemed necessary to have a military presence on hand that could be mobilized quickly. But even so, such governors interfered little in local affairs unless it became necessary to do so. They were responsible for seeing that the tribute was paid and peace maintained in the territory. They also had the power to execute lawbreakers. But most internal issues were left in the hands of the local governing bodies. In the case of Judea, this meant that the Sanhedrin and the high priest—essentially stripped of authority under Herod the Great—were once again empowered to order civil affairs.

Between AD 6 and AD 41, Judea was administered by six or seven different governors. We know little about their administrations, with one exception: Pontius Pilate (AD 26–36). Josephus depicts Pilate as a cruel, greedy, insensitive man.[9] He began offending the Jews on his first entry into Jerusalem. Because the Jews were so opposed to graven images (interpreted broadly), prior Roman governors had instructed their troops to lower their standards—which were emblazoned with images of animals, and almost treated like icons by the Roman soldiers—before entering Jerusalem. But Pilate ignored the custom. Instead, he had his troops enter the city with their standards held high, and they planted them right in front of the Temple. When a crowd of Jews gathered and demanded the removal of the offensive flags, Pilate threatened to kill them all if they did not disperse. But instead of dispersing, the Jews threw themselves to the ground and bared their necks, saying they preferred to die than see their Temple desecrated. Pilate grudgingly removed the standards. But later, he further offended the Jews by appropriating Temple funds to build an aqueduct. The crowds who gathered to protest the action were beaten, and many perished. He also insulted his subjects by placing votive shields with the Emperor's name engraved on them within the Temple itself. He was officially reprimanded by Rome more than once, and threatened with exile. The last straw came a few years after Jesus' death. In AD 35, a prophet promised to make the vessels of the Temple (taken away by the Babylonians during the Exile) miraculously appear on Mt. Gerizim in Samaria. A huge crowd of Samaritans gathered to witness the event. Pilate, however, suspected that the gathering would erupt in rebellion, so he ordered his soldiers to attack the group and kill its leaders. The Samaritans lodged a formal protest with the governor of Syria, and Pilate was recalled to Rome.

With the administrations of Antipas and Pilate, we come to the end of the era of Jesus' earthly ministry. In the next chapter, we will examine how these developments shaped the political situation in Judea during the time of Jesus.

---

9. Ant. 18:55–62, 85–89; War 1:169–177.

5

The Government

THE HISTORICAL EVENTS WE have surveyed produced a geographical landscape unlike any the world had ever known. It was, we might say, remarkably flat. The conquests of Alexander and the Romans imposed what we might call a political homogeneity on the world. No more was Judah a small kingdom fighting for its life against Philistines, Edomites, Assyrians, Egyptians, Babylonians, and Syrians. The national rivalries of Old Testament times were a distant memory. The only competing powers in Judea's landscape were the Romans and the Parthians. Rome and Parthia had negotiated a truce in 20 BC, and the Parthians played little part in Judean affairs during Jesus' lifetime. Politically at least, the world was blissfully uncomplicated.

THE ROMAN EMPIRE

The Roman Empire, contrary to common conception, was not an autocracy run according to the whims of a single individual. Its government was similar in structure to the government of the United States. There was an elected legislature—the Senate—that was technically in charge of running Rome and its environs. Then there was the Emperor, the "first citizen" of Rome, whose power was officially exercised primarily outside of Italy.

To understand the relationship between the Emperor and the Senate, it is necessary to know a little about the history of Rome's conquests. In the fourth and third centuries BC, when Rome had not yet officially become an "empire" (because it had no emperor), the Roman Republic had expanded its influence throughout the Italian peninsula by a combination of military might and diplomacy. In order to build a sense of unity, the conquered territories were officially incorporated into the

Republic, with all the rights and responsibilities of Roman citizenship. But when Rome took Sicily from Carthage in 241 BC, it faced a new situation. Sicily was not part of the Italian peninsula, and so Rome was disinclined to bequeath on its residents the privileges of citizenship. And so, the Romans developed a new status for this land: it was deemed the first Roman "province," a designation that would be applied henceforth to all conquered lands. A Roman governor was placed over the land as its chief administrator. The natives were required to pay heavy tribute to their overlords, but administrative affairs were generally left in the hands of the locals, as long Roman interests were not threatened.

But it was not just foreigners who were "second class citizens" in the Roman Republic. In Rome itself, there was a rigid caste system that became a source of massive unrest. Rome's military conquests were creating new opportunities for those of the lower class, known as the *plebs*. As their economic clout increased, the members of this class believed their political and social position should improve, as well. The upper classes, however, were reluctant to share their status. The tensions resulted in riots. In 85 BC, the Roman general Sulla took it upon himself to violently squash a plebian uprising and impose martial law on Rome. But once he had restored order to the capital, he relinquished power back into the hands of the Roman Senate. In the decades to follow, it became apparent that the only way to maintain order, even in Rome itself, was through a strong military. In this setting, ambitious and competent generals prospered. They had something of a love-hate relationship with the Senate, which feared their power but needed their ominous threat to keep the masses in line.

Julius Caesar's attempt to seize control of Rome ended in his assassination in 45 BC. The Senate then attempted to squelch the growing power and influence of the generals, but to no avail. When Mark Antony formed his alliance with Cleopatra, Caesar's nephew, General Octavian, managed to persuade the Senate that Antony and Egypt were a dire threat to Rome itself. The Senate granted Octavian extensive emergency powers to meet the crisis. Once Antony and Cleopatra were subdued and order was restored to Rome, Octavian voluntarily relinquished the powers that had been granted to him. The grateful Senate rewarded Octavian in 27 BC by declaring him emperor and bequeathing on him the title "Augustus" (Exalted One). Technically, the Senate was still in charge of non-military affairs in Rome itself, and many of the provinces were under senatorial jurisdiction. The Emperor's authority was primarily limited to the provinces placed under his command (Egypt, Gaul, Hispania and Coele-Syria) and to military matters.[1] But practically, the Emperor was the most powerful man both in and outside of Rome. The Senate was essentially irrelevant to the affairs of Palestine.

THE EMPEROR

Jesus was born during the reign of the first emperor, Augustus. Augustus's stabilization of Roman politics and his restoration of traditional values to Roman society have earned him a lasting place in history. But for our purposes, the most important aspect of his reign was the impact he had on the Near East. Augustus was responsible for the institution of the famous *pax Romana*—the Peace of Rome. He put down piracy on the Mediterranean, making the way safe for merchant vessels. He built roads for the movement of his armies and for the easy congress of caravans from the East. The roads were patrolled by Roman troops, helping to assure the safe conduct of goods and people throughout the realm. And he enforced a strict policy that none of the nations in his provinces were allowed to wage war against another without his permission. As a result of these practices, people and news could spread freely throughout Palestine. Jesus was surely no world traveler like St. Paul, but the Roman Empire made it safe for him to travel the roads of Galilee, and even to pass through the land of Samaria. Furthermore, this sense of security encouraged great audiences of pilgrims to flock to the Galilean prophet, feeling no reluctance to travel through the formerly treacherous highways between Judea and Galilee.

Augustus also reformed the system of taxation in the provinces, which had been a source of great discontent. As part of the privilege of being "citizens of Rome," the people of Italy were not taxed. This fact meant that the burden for financing the Empire fell on the provinces. To Rome, this arrangement must have seemed fair: all Romans were required to serve in the military, while people living in the provinces were exempted from military draft (they could volunteer for service if they desired, but Romans generally felt that foreigners made inferior soldiers). While locals could be conscripted to perform manual labor

---

1. The phrase Coele-Syria was the Roman designation for the lands of Syria and Palestine. It was probably a Latin corruption of the Aramaic phrase meaning "All of Syria."

for the Roman legions or to provide them lodging for a night, they did not generally fight for the defense and expansion of the Empire. Since the people of the provinces benefited from the sacrifices of full Roman citizens, should they not do their "fair share" to assure that the government ran smoothly? But unfortunately, taxation in the provinces was seldom administered fairly. Both Roman officials and local tax collectors—the *publicani*—were equally guilty of exploiting their offices and the provincials to the fullest. (Among the Jews, the "publicans" had the further stigma of being collaborators with the oppressors and of dealing in the currency of the Empire, which featured a graven image of the Emperor.) When Antony had been fighting Octavian and trying to impress Cleopatra, he almost bled the Asian provinces dry. So by Augustus's day, the East was no longer able to provide the revenue it once had, and the loss of income was threatening the stability of the entire Empire. Augustus made little change in the rate of taxation, but he instituted policies to improve the methods of collection, to reduce graft, and distribute the tax burden more equitably.

Augustus's activities eventually resulted in greater prosperity for many people in the Empire, including the Jews. The average person may have been more comfortable than ever before in history, enjoying the fruits of Rome's conquests and its far-flung commercial interests. The affluence of this era surely left its mark on Jesus' preaching. Love of money was becoming a growing problem, even among such normally austere people as the Pharisees, who were becoming addicted to the latest luxuries. Jesus spoke frequently on the subject of money, warning his listeners of the dangers of hoarding wealth (e.g., Luke 12:13–21; 16:19–31).

The people of Judea rarely had any direct dealings with the Emperor. The main source of potential conflict was in the imperial cult: the worship of the Emperor as the embodiment of the spirit Rome. This practice will be discussed in Chapter 7.

ADMINISTRATION OF THE PROVINCES

There was a good deal of flexibility in how Rome administered the provinces, and the amount of autonomy given to local leaders varied widely. Before Herod was named its king, Judea was under the administration of the governor of Coele-Syria. Following the typical Roman practice, the governor appointed native officials to handle all local administration. For the most part, the governor's major concerns were to see that taxes were paid and peace was maintained. The governors were typically prominent Romans from the upper classes of Roman society, the equestrians (the "knight" class) and the patricians (politician class). These appointments were usually considered very desirable, and a necessary stepping stone for those who had designs on becoming senators. It cost money to become a politician in Rome, and provincial governance was a place where money could be made. Remarkably, the most troubled provinces—those with the greatest potential for violence—were the most sought-after. These provinces offered the possibility for war, and war meant the spoils of war: property to confiscate, slaves to sell, and the glory of victory. There were long waiting lists for provincial appointments, and a great deal of turnover in the offices.

When the Roman Senate made Herod the Great king of Judea, Judea became an allied kingdom. Such "client kingdoms" were generally allowed to run their own affairs with their native monarchy in place. This state of affairs existed when the Romans found the existing rulers to be especially useful, or administration of the land would seem especially problematic. There was no hard and fast policy regarding these kingdoms or their rights and responsibilities. Rome interfered little in Judean affairs, except for Antony's meddling at the instigation of Cleopatra. After Augustus became emperor, Herod was mostly free to run the kingdom as he saw fit, not even answering to the local governor. Herod was required to see that tribute was paid to Rome; he could wage war only with Roman consent; he was required to provide military assistance to Rome when requested. But otherwise, the kingdom was essentially independent.

After Herod's death, however, the kingdom was divided and placed under the administration of his sons, who were not granted the rank of "king." Judea was no longer an allied kingdom, but part of the Syrian province, and the Herodides (sons of Herod) were officially subordinate to the Roman governor of Coele-Syria. (Such changes in status were not unusual in the Empire.) Apparently the governor of Coele-Syria had limited authority over them, however, since when the Jews and Samaritans had complaints against Archelaus and Herod Antipas, they were taken directly to the emperor and not to the local official.

After Archelaus was deposed as governor of Judea in AD 6, Judea was designated an "imperial procuratorial province" and placed under the administration of a Roman governor. Even though this position officially answered directly to the emperor, the "prefect," as he was known in this era, clearly operated in subordination to the governor of Coele-Syria. When the people of Samaria wanted Pontius Pilate removed from office in AD 35, they lodged their complaint with the governor of Coele-Syria, and it was he who brought their concerns before the emperor.

THE PREFECTS

The prefects of Judea received their appointments from the Emperor. We know little about most of them, since neither the New Testament nor Josephus have much to say about their administrations. As a general rule, the prefects during this era seem to have allowed the Jews to manage their own affairs. They did not consider it their job to tell the locals how to live. As long as the taxes were paid, the people were pacified, and their own pockets were well lined, the prefects allowed native officials to handle most internal matters.

There was, however, a great deal of latitude allowed in the way they carried out their responsibilities. Pontius Pilate, the only prefect of this era about whom we know much of anything, took more of a strong-arm approach. It was apparently within his power to overrule the local officials or deprive them of some authority, if he felt it would insure the peace and prosperity of the realm. In situations that called for a strong hand, the prefects might even impose martial law and do away with local administration entirely. In these cases, the natives might present a formal complaint to the ranking regional official or to the emperor. If Rome determined that the governor had overstepped his bounds, he could be disciplined with anything from an official reprimand to exile in one of the many less-pleasant backwaters of the Empire.

THE SANHEDRIN

Local matters in Judea were generally administered by the Sanhedrin. The name "Sanhedrin" is Greek for "assembly." (In Hebrew and Aramaic literature, the usual title for this institution is *bet din*, meaning "House of Judgment.") Though the Assembly is most commonly known by its Greek name, the institution undoubtedly goes back to early biblical times. Informal councils of elders are a common feature of tribal societies, and this institution was formalized as Israel became more organized. In the Old Testament, we read of Moses placing judges over the people

(Exod 18:17-26) and assembling a council of seventy elders to help him judge the people of Israel (Num 11:16-17, 24-30). In Psalms we read of "the council of the elders" (Psa 107:32), and the prophet Ezekiel had a vision in which "the seventy elders of the house of Israel" committed idolatry in the Temple (Ezek 8:11). After the destruction of Judah's monarchy, the council of elders assumed an even more formal leadership role (see Ezra 5:5). The council of elders was apparently the most persistent institution of leadership in Judah, originating in antiquity and continuing uninterrupted until it was abolished by the Romans in the second century AD.

The national Sanhedrin of Jerusalem is sometimes known as the Great Sanhedrin, in order to distinguish it from local assemblies known by the same name. According to rabbinic tradition, it consisted of seventy adult males plus its president, and there is some evidence that this tradition is reliable (see, e.g., Josephus *War* 2:482; 2:570; 4:341). Some scholars believe, however, that this number was simply based on the Old Testament passages referenced above rather than historical reality. In the time of Jesus, the Sanhedrin might have been an *ad hoc* association, without a formal chartered membership. The constituents were selected from the priestly and scribal sectors of the community. It is unclear how the members of the council were selected, but there is no reason to doubt that there were serious politics involved in the process. Through most of the Hasmonean era, the Sanhedrin was comprised primarily of Sadducees, the favored sect of the day, but the balance apparently had swung to the Pharisees during the reign of Alexandra Salome. In New Testament times, there seems to have been a fair mix of both groups represented (see Acts 23:6-8). Apparently there was a certain amount of wealth required, as well: Nicodemus and Joseph of Arimathea are both identified as members of the Sanhedrin (Luke 23:50; John 3:1), and both seem to have been more affluent members of Judean society (Matt 27:57; John 19:38-39).

The president of the Sanhedrin apparently had the power to convene the body and acted as its spokesman, but his vote carried no more weight than that of the other council members. According to both Josephus (*Ant.* 20:251) and the New Testament (Matt 26:62-66; Mark 14:53-63; Acts 23:1-5), the high priest served as the president of the Great Sanhedrin. This statement is at odds with rabbinic tradition found in the Talmud, which holds that the Sanhedrin was chaired by an official called the *nasi* ("prince"), and that the office was held by the great rabbi Hillel and his disciples until the second century AD (*b. Shabb.* 15a). The rabbinic tradition, written several hundred years after the fact, probably represents an idealization of the situation, projecting the later rabbinic authority back on to earlier times. (There is also a slim possibility that the rabbis are referring to an informal assembly of Pharisaic leaders, rather than the official Sanhedrin of Jerusalem.) In general, the rabbinic traditions seem to cast the first-century Sanhedrin in a more positive light than it deserves. Both the New Testament and Josephus make it clear that the high priests in this period were often scoundrels, appointed by the governors because of their political connections rather than their piety. Josephus even tells of one high priest depriving the other priests of their due portion of the tithes and offerings, driving some of them to starvation.

We do not know much about how trials were conducted in the time of Jesus, and only a few facts can be gleaned from the Bible and Josephus's accounts. The Mishnah, especially chapter 4 of the tractate *Sanhedrin*, contains some detailed descriptions of the proceedings for local trials, as well as some comments about the Great Sanhedrin. As always, however, these sources must be regarded critically. According to several rabbinic passages, the Great Sanhedrin convened in a room adjoining the Temple known as the "Hall of Hewn Stones" (this title distinguished it from the holy precincts of the Temple, which was constructed of stones that had not been worked by human implements). Josephus, however, seems to imply the council was located near a structure called the Xystus, which was situated to the west of the Temple Mount (*War* 5:144). The Mishnah reports that in local courts, the members of the council sat in a semicircle so they could see each other while deliberating, with two clerks standing before them to record the vote (*m. Sanh.* 4:3). For criminal trials, a quorum of twenty-three members was required in order to proceed.

Accusations could be brought forward by a private individual, or the Sanhedrin itself might order the arrest of suspected criminals. The accused was to appear before the Sanhedrin with humble demeanor, dressed in mourning garb (Jos. *Ant.* 14:172). First the defense would present its case, then the prosecution. Old Testament law stipulated that no one could be convicted on the testimony of a single witness (Deut 19:15), and that policy persisted into New Testament times and beyond. Two witnesses, or better three, were required for a conviction. A majority of one vote was sufficient for acquittal, but a two-vote majority was required for conviction. The Great Sanhedrin could be convened on any day but the Sabbath or a feast day. In a trial for a capital offence, an acquittal was announced as soon as the verdict had been rendered. A guilty verdict, on the other hand, would not be announced until the following morning.

The power of the Sanhedrin varied in different times, depending on who was ruling the nation. The Hasmonean Alexander Janneus gutted its authority; his widow and successor Alexandra Salome allowed it to carry out witch hunts against its enemies. During the administration of Hyrcanus II, the Sanhedrin felt empowered to summon the governor of Galilee (Herod) to stand trial; during the reign of Herod the Great, the Sanhedrin was relegated to the function of a religious tribunal only, without the power to enforce its rulings. The Roman prefects seem to have allowed the Sanhedrin to handle most all of Judea's internal affairs. When Pontius Pilate was prefect, however, it was apparently deprived of the right to execute criminals (John 18:31).

In addition to the Great Sanhedrin, there were local sanhedrins that could decide various affairs and infractions. This practice, too, has a long pedigree: the Old Testament often refers to "the elders of the town" who made decisions or acted as representatives of the people (e.g., Judg 8:14, 11:5; Ruth 4:2; 1 Kgs 21:8). Rabbinic teachings attempted to standardize the tradition. According to the Mishnah, any town with more than 120 adult males could have a sanhedrin comprised of twenty-three men. Rabbinic tradition seems to assume that local councils could try most crimes that the Great Sanhedrin could hear, with a few exceptions: only the Great Sanhedrin could try a false prophet or a high priest; it alone could order a war of conquest; it could change the boundaries of the Temple or Jerusalem; and it alone could establish lesser sanhedrins (*m. Sanh.* 1:5). Also, decisions of the local councils could be appealed to the Great Sanhedrin.

ENFORCING THE LAW

The Empire could impose taxes and discourage insurrection, and the Sanhedrin could interpret laws and try criminals. But how were these policies enacted? Who was responsible for enforcement? There were no policemen in ancient Judea. There was no local sheriff. Law enforcement was very different in the ancient world than from our day: it was often the responsibility of the community, rather than some select individuals. The entire town would bring lawbreakers out to the authorities. The whole community would know and abide by the decisions of the councils. If someone was to be stoned to death, all the men would gather and participate in the execution together. There was thus a corporate ownership of justice that is largely missing in modern western society.

The primary protectors of peace and justice in the Roman Empire were the armies. Judea had a national militia, but since the provincial kingdoms were not allowed to make war without Rome's approval, it received little practice. Herod and his sons maintained their own armies, but those forces were probably disbanded under the Roman governors, who would not have trusted Judean troops. Instead, they would have made use of the Roman troops garrisoned at Caesarea. Few Roman troops would have been stationed in Jerusalem regularly, or in the other Judean cities. They would only have been brought in when necessary to put down trouble, so the average Jew had little contact with Roman soldiers. There was, however, a regular contingent of troops in the Temple, which served as a repository of precious religious objects and as a bank for private individuals. These soldiers were at the disposal of the Sanhedrin and the high priest, as when they were sent forth to arrest Jesus in Gethsemane.

FORMS OF PUNISHMENT

Punishments for lawbreakers would be considered severe by modern standards. Under Jewish law, property crimes generally were punished with stiff fines (see Exod 2:1). In Jesus' day, incarceration—a form of punishment unknown in the Old Testament—could also be imposed, but often this was a temporary measure to detain someone prior to their trial rather than the punishment itself. In the Old Testament, a number of crimes were to be punished by expulsion from the community (see, e.g., Lev 20:18). The Talmud implies that this policy was still enforced in New Testament times. Many crimes, however, were considered too minor to deem such a severe punishment. For many infractions, such as extortion, eating non-kosher food, or being a general nuisance, a court could impose a beating with whips. Among the Jews, this punishment was practiced with great restraint. The Bible commands that no more than forty lashes could be given to an Israelite, because he was to be considered a brother (Deut 25:3). The idea here was to correct and redeem the person. After the punishment was given, the penitent souls were to be welcomed back into the community. In Jesus' day, the maximum number of lashes given was thirty-nine (see 2 Cor 11:24). The thought here was to provide a margin of error, so that the Israelites would not even come close to breaking the Law. (The Mishnah calls setting up of such margins "building a hedge around the Law." [*m. Aboth* 1:1.] It was a basic principle behind the Pharisaic, and later rabbinic, approaches to the Law.) The Romans, however, had no such restraints. It was not uncommon for them to whip criminals to death with the *flagellum*, a corded whip outfitted with pieces of sharp bone or pottery that could literally tear the skin from the body.

Capital punishment was regularly practiced by the Jews, though apparently the Roman governors sometimes restricted this right (as noted previously). The Old Testament prescribed capital punishment for a wide variety of crimes, but in Jesus' day, the Jewish courts seem to have imposed the death sentence only rarely. The Jews by this period were not a nomadic people requiring instant dispensing of justice, and they had adopted many of the more lenient attitudes of Hellenism (see Chapter 6). While they might be scandalized by (say) a brother and sister cohabitating, they did not demand the death of the offenders. Even rabbinic attitudes were quite liberal on criminal penalties, developing methods of biblical interpretation that permitted them a good deal of leeway in their application of the biblical injunctions. For example, the requirements of the so-called *lex talionis*, "An eye for an eye, tooth for tooth" (Lev 24:19–20), were replaced with monetary compensation for inadvertent injuries (*b. B. Qam.* 83b—84a).

Even so, there were three crimes that the Jews found so offensive that they commonly drew the ultimate penalty. Murder always was punishable by death. Adultery frequently drew this penalty, but there was more opportunity for leniency. Blasphemy was a tricky matter: in the age of religious pluralism, it would be difficult to define blasphemy to everyone's satisfaction (rabbinic tradition stated that blasphemy had to involve using the divine name in an insulting manner). But it seems that this charge was sometimes invoked as a convenient way of removing dangerous people. Also, Gentiles who entered the precincts of the Temple reserved for Jews were subject to the death penalty. Of course, Roman officials would add insurrection to this list of capital offences, even though the Jewish authorities might be willing in many circumstances to overlook such activities.

Judean officials could execute lawbreakers by burning at the stake (*m. Sanh.* 7:2), or they might strangle them, as Herod had executed his wife and sons. But the usual Jewish method of execution was stoning. Stoning could take either of two forms: a person could be pushed from a cliff to their death, or they could be pummeled with stones until they died. In either case, all the men of the community served as the executioners. (There were no specialists in the dealing of death.) The body of the criminal could then be hung or impaled on a stake as a deterrent, but Jewish law forbid crucifixion as a form of execution (see Deut 21:22). Only one Jewish monarch ever employed crucifixion against his enemies: the depraved Hasmonean Alexander Janneus (Jos. *Ant.* 13:380).

CRUCIFIXION

The Romans practiced a variety of forms of execution. Roman citizens would be "honored" with beheading, a quick and relatively painless (we assume) manner of death. Non-citizens and slaves could be dispatched in many creative ways: gladiatorial combat, lions, and burning at the stake were all accepted ways of punishing lawbreakers and creating a public spectacle in the process. But the most infamous method of execution among the Romans was crucifixion. It was not a Roman invention, having been practiced by the Persians and Seleucids before them. Among the Romans, the method was usually reserved for slaves, insurrectionists, bandits, or other particularly unpleasant cases. Crucifixion was designed to be the ultimate deterrent.

The purpose to crucifixion was not only to torture the victims, but also to heap humiliation on them. The crosses were erected on busy streets where they were sure to garner attention. They could be quite short, so that the passers-by would get a good look at the criminals. Mocking and abusing the helpless men were encouraged. The prisoners were stripped naked and generally beaten with the *flagellum* before being crucified. Such a treatment in itself could often bring about the death of the prisoner. The actual method of crucifixion varied considerably. The cross itself took different forms, from the traditional "t" shape, to an "x" shape, to a simple upright pole. If the cross had a horizontal member, the prisoner was forced to carry the beam (which might weigh between 75–125 pounds) to the place of execution, where the upright would already be in place. The condemned might be nailed to the cross, or they might simply be bound. In some cases, both ropes and nails were used.

Nails could be put through the palms or through the wrists (if the victim was bound, the flesh would not have to carry the weight of the body). A single nail might be used to secure both ankles. The condemned were crucified in any number of positions, with arms spread or straight above their heads, legs straight or bent, spread-eagle, or even upside-down. The Roman writer Seneca even reports victims being impaled through their groins. A plaque, called a *titulus*, was nailed over the victims' heads with their name and crime—"Gaius Stephanus: Bandit"; "Hezekiah ben Mattathias: Murderer"—to discourage anyone who might have aspirations of following a similar life of crime. Death came to the prisoners slowly, often over a period of several days.

There has been some speculation on how the victims of crucifixion actually died. Those who were simply bound to the crosses probably died of thirst and exposure after prolonged suffering. For those nailed to the crosses, death could come more swiftly. One popular theory holds that the crucified died of asphyxiation due to hyperextension of the lungs. In experimental studies, however, individuals suspended with their arms extended experienced no difficulty in breathing. Most likely, victims died of shock, loss of blood, dehydration, or exposure. Sometimes, the victims' legs were broken with a club in a procedure called *crurifragium*. This procedure hastened death (see John 13:31–32), perhaps by inducing shock or causing embolisms; but it also added to the torment, and served to make the spectacle even more of a deterrent.

Bodies of crucified victims were disposed of in many ways. Often, corpses of ignominious individuals would be left on the cross to decay, or they were dumped on trash heaps, where they might be devoured by wild animals. Given the emphasis on honor and shame in ancient Mediterranean societies, most families would not have come forward to claim the body of someone who had committed a crime worthy of crucifixion. Among the Jews, however, there was a strong emphasis placed on the proper burial of the dead, even if they had been executed (the apocryphal Book of Tobit well illustrates the importance of this custom to the Jewish people). It was quite possible that desire to give the dead a proper burial outweighed shame, and that Jewish victims might have regularly been recovered for proper burial. In 1968, a body was discovered in Jerusalem of a man who had been crucified and his remains preserved in an ossuary (bone box, see Chapter 6).[2] The family was willing

2. See Tzaferis, "Crucifixion."

to bear the indignation of claiming a convicted criminal for the sake of providing their loved one with a proper burial. In this case, we know the man was a victim of crucifixion because the nail that had been placed in his ankles was buried with the body, because it had been bent and could not be removed. It is entirely possible that there were other victims of crucifixion buried in Jewish tombs, but because of their poor state of preservation, they have not been identified.

6

The Cultural Context

MANY MODERN MEN AND women like to believe that all people of the world are basically the same. There is surely a grain of truth in the sentiment, since we all share the same biology and many of the same values. But on the other hand, there are also numerous differences between the peoples of various geographical regions and ethnic groups. There are different languages, different customs, and different values. There are also technological differences, especially when we are considering ancient civilizations. All these features of society constitute what we call "culture."

We will not attempt to present a comprehensive account of Jesus' cultural background in this little book. First of all, culture is simply too vast a phenomenon for us to cover in all its many facets. A comprehensive discussion of all the features of daily life, of family relations, of religious observance, etc., that constitute the cultural aspects of Jesus' world would fill several volumes. But on the other hand, we really do not know that much about the culture of the ancient Palestinian rural class to which Jesus belonged. Historical and literary accounts are usually written by (and about) the urban elites, not the people of small towns in Galilee. Often, the villagers were illiterate, but even those who were able to read had little reason to do much writing. Also, writing materials were not cheap in those days, so the words and thoughts of the common folk have been mostly lost to us. Furthermore, most of the artifacts that have been discovered have come from the urban centers, not the villages, because those are the areas where archeologists have concentrated their efforts. So while we have far more information than we can possibly present, there is still much that we would like to know that we simply have not been able to discover, given the nature of our sources.

Instead of trying to survey the culture of Jewish world in the time of Jesus, we will only consider some of the most cogent points for understanding the Gospels' presentation of Jesus' life and ministry, while filling out the picture in other volumes of this series. We will proceed here from broad to specific, starting with the general Mediterranean context and the shared culture of the Roman world. We will then focus on the East, and the unique features of the Near Eastern culture. We will finally devote the bulk of the chapter to the unique features of Palestinian Jewish culture. In popular treatments of this era, we frequently find a failure to distinguish between practices that are uniquely Jewish and those that are common to the Near East, or even to ancient civilizations in general. But when we acknowledge the cultural universals of the era, the unique features of Jewish society stand out in even greater relief.

THE COMMON CULTURE OF THE ROMAN EMPIRE

Millennia before the time of Jesus, the diverse peoples surrounding the Mediterranean Sea had already begun to have many cultural traits in common. These shared qualities came from a variety of sources: the common climate shaped diet and clothing styles; trade had been conducted across the Mediterranean from time immemorial, facilitating the exchange of goods and ideas; migrations and slave sales brought diverse ethnic groups into face-to-face contact. As a result, we find Persian and Aramaic words in Roman texts, and Greek words in the Hebrew Bible. We find a common alphabet used by all the people of the Mediterranean world, thanks to the Phoenician merchants who wanted to facilitate record keeping. Stories spread from land to land, adapting to local language and customs. For instance, in Babylon, the young vegetation god who died and was restored to life was known as Tammuz, but the Egyptians called the same god Osiris, while the Greeks called him Adonis. The stories differ in details, but the basic myth is the same. The diverse Mediterranean peoples even held some superstitions in common: for example, the Greeks might have read astrological treatises written by the Babylonians, and Roman exorcists might have recited chants incorporating the name of the Jewish God in order to drive out evil spirits. It seems like it was a small world, even though it could take months to travel from one end of the Roman Empire to the other.

HONOR AND SHAME

One of the most significant of these universal qualities was a shared sense of honor and shame. Honor might be defined as the recognition and appreciation of one's standing in the community. Shame, on the other hand, is a lack of appreciation for someone's place. Those who acted in ways appropriate for their standing, or perhaps even for those of higher standing, could bring honor upon themselves. Those who acted in a manner inappropriate for their "place," or who were treated in ways that were beneath their station, would be shamed. For people of the ancient Mediterranean region, honor was supremely important, more important than life itself. "Death before dishonor" is not just a battle cry of a comic book action hero. It was a very real principle by which most people of Jesus' world lived their lives. When the 300 Spartans stood against the forces of the Persian King Xerxes at the Battle of Thermopylae Pass in 480 BC, all but one lost their lives. The survivor killed himself rather than bear the shame of living when his comrades had the honor of dying in battle.

Much of how a person conducted their daily life was directly related to acquiring honor and avoiding shame. If someone was invited to a neighbor's home for dinner, he would be expected to reciprocate with an equal or more lavish affair, or he would be shamed. A parent whose children were disobedient was publicly shamed by his or her children, so harsh discipline was often the rule (see Deut 21:18–21). Performing religious rituals was a very public affair, since it could bring honor to the worshipper. Charity or gifts were given with much fanfare, since the ability to give large gifts was a source of honor. In general, people judged themselves by what others thought of them, and few people would risk behaving in ways that their peers might deem inappropriate. It was uncommon for people to hide their light under a bushel. In fact, bragging was considered a very natural form of discourse. Modern readers can find ancient writers quite immodest and not a little annoying.

There could be many different bases for one's honor, and not everyone expected or received honor in the same measure. Family background was an important source of honor, and the heroic deeds of one's ancestors would be preserved in stories that would be told to anyone who would listen. Certain professions were considered more honorable than others. In Judea, priests received more honor than bricklayers or farmers; in Sparta, soldiering was considered the only honorable career for an adult male. Elders were universally considered to be worthy of honor, and mocking old people was considered extremely deplorable conduct (see, e.g., Gen 9:20–27; Lev 19:32). Adult men were more worthy of honor than women or children; fathers were more deserving of honor than childless men. Each individual knew his or her expected honor in society, and frustrating those expectations could result in dire consequences. Indeed, someone who felt they had been dishonored might well respond violently to the insult.

KINSHIP

In the ancient Mediterranean region, the primary way one defined his or her place in society was through kinship. Kinship refers to norms of behavior and self-identification based on family relations. When someone was introduced in the ancient Roman world, they usually would not be identified primarily by their profession or alma mater, as we might be in our day ("This is Bob the baker." "Meet George. He's a Yale man."). Rather, it was their parentage and bloodline that was the foremost concern: "Here is Simon, son of Jonas." "This is Alexander of the Hasmonean clan."

Strictly speaking, family connections could be established in three ways: by birth, adoption, or marriage. Birth, of course, is obvious. Genealogies were carefully recorded and preserved as a means of demonstrating the prestige of one's bloodline. Adoption was a common practice throughout all the realms of the Roman Empire. It could be used as a way of providing children to childless families, of caring for orphans (usually children of relatives), or as a way of conferring the family's honor on the adopted child (as when Octavian, later to become the emperor Augustus, was adopted by Julius Caesar). There is no explicit mention of adoption in the Hebrew Bible, but the practice was common in the ancient Near East, and there is no reason to doubt that the Jewish people adopted children, as later tradition affirms (see *b. Sanh.* 119b). Marriages intertwined families far more thoroughly than we can imagine today, since extended families lived together in close proximity, often under the same roof. Because family ties were so fundamental to a person's self-definition, marriages to relatives (such as cousins or nieces) were often encouraged. It was the extended family, not the nuclear family, which was the foundation of society.

In addition to these obvious family ties, there were other ways that the significance of kinship manifested itself in the ancient world. One way is the identification of individuals by their town of origin. Often in small towns, there were extensive interconnections between nuclear or extended families through marriage, so one's hometown was also one's family group. Joseph of Arimathea was clearly a resident of Jerusalem, since he had a family tomb there, but his association with Arimathea undoubtedly said a great deal about his family background to those who knew him. Also, the people of the ancient Mediterranean regions put much stock in genealogies rooted in tradition rather than historically verifiable facts. Alexander the Great, for instance, claimed to be descended from Achilles. During the Hasmonean Revolt, the Jews placed much emphasis on their (fictional) kinship with the Spartans.

HELLENISM

Yet another universal feature of Roman imperial society was Hellenism, or Greek cultural influence. When Alexander the Great had come to Asia, his dream had been to demonstrate the superiority of Greek culture and impose a new way of life on the eastern barbarians. But he had not gotten far in this crusade before his imperial vision began to change. The East cast its spell on the great conqueror, and seduced him with its opulence and pageantry. Alexander soon had a new mission: a merger of East and West into a bold new culture, a culture that embraced the best of both worlds. As mentioned earlier, Alexander symbolized the union with a mass wedding in the city of Susa (a capital of Persia), where 324 of his officers and 10,000 of his soldiers married Asian women at a ceremony presided over by both Greek and Persian priests. But it seemed Alexander's new world would be stillborn. When Alexander died, most of his officers divorced their native wives and took Greek women instead. The Ptolemies of Egypt subjugated the natives and poured favor on the Greek and Macedonian expatriates in their land. Throughout the Seleucid Empire of Syria, cities that adopted Greek styles of government and education were exempted from taxation. The native culture, it seemed, was to be supplanted by the "superior" ways of the Greeks.

But reports of the death of "Orientalism" had been greatly exaggerated. The East wooed Alexander's successors, and before long, they were adopting many of the trappings of eastern potentates. Native culture, too, proved far more resilient than the Greeks would have believed. True, there were natives who drank deep at the well of Western culture. There were "wannabes" who sought to look and act as much like their

Greek overlords as possible. There were some natives who were completely assimilated to the culture of their conquerors. But there were also pockets where it was almost as if the Greeks had never come. Especially in the rural areas, there was little need, and little desire, for the natives to abandon their traditional ways to adopt the ways of the West.

Nonetheless, the influence of Greek culture on the Roman Empire was undeniable and generally pervasive. As we discuss some aspects Palestinian Jewish culture below, we will observe several ways in which Hellenism left its mark on Jesus' countryfolk. But the entire Mediterranean world was affected by some aspects of this powerful cultural force.

LANGUAGE

Hellenism made its presence felt most deeply in the area of international relations. Unlike the Persians, who had allowed the western regions of their empire to use the familiar Aramaic language they had adopted during the days of the Babylonian Empire, the Macedonian conquerors insisted that all business of state be conducted in Greek. There were obvious advantages to the arrangement: international relations regularly stretched across the Mediterranean to Greece, Macedon, and to Greek colonies in various areas. It certainly simplified matters to have everyone able to communicate in the same language. So Greek became the *lingua franca* of the Mediterranean world. Anyone who wanted to be taken seriously by the Greek overlords had to be able to read and speak Greek. Furthermore, anyone who wanted to be able to expand their business in the new international milieu had to be able to use Greek as well. In Egypt, Asia Minor, Syria, and of course Palestine, many natives became skilled in the language. For many people, even for Jews living outside Palestine, Greek became their first language. Of course, that does not mean that *all* the Jews learned to speak Greek. In fact, even an upper-class cosmopolitan Jew like Josephus admitted that he was not very skilled in the use of Greek (*Against Apion* 1:9). When he wrote his first account of the Jewish revolt, he needed assistants to help with the subtleties of the language. But on the other hand, a cultured Diaspora Jew like Philo was as facile in Greek as any native speaker.

Scholars have long debated how extensive the use of Greek was among the Palestinian Jews. In the big cities, there was possibly a good deal of knowledge of the Greek language. Many Greek inscriptions have been discovered that were obviously produced by (or for) Jews in the cities of Syria-Palestine. In the small towns and countryside, however, the traditional languages persisted. The Jews' ancestral tongue, Hebrew, was still spoken by some segments of society, as numerous artifacts and inscriptions have demonstrated. While its everyday use may have been limited by this era, it was the preferred language for religious and patriotic text or inscriptions. But Aramaic, the Semitic language adopted by many Jews during the Babylonian Exile, was clearly the most common tongue of the Palestinian Jews. Several Aramaic words and phrases even made their way into the (Greek) New Testament: "*Talitha, qumi*" ("Maiden, arise"); "*Ephratha*" ("Open"); "*Abba*" ("My Father"); "*maranatha*" (Our Lord, Come"). From quotations in the Gospels, it is clear that Jesus generally spoke Aramaic, but did he know Greek as well? Some of the cities of Galilee had substantial Gentile populations, but as noted in Chapter 3, studies have demonstrated that the Greek presence was not nearly as pervasive as once believed. The population of the region was overwhelmingly Jewish. While a major city like Sepphoris, with its population of approximately 10,000 inhabitants, may well have had Greek residents, evidence for their presence there in the first century AD is scant—while evidence of Jewish presence is abundant. Jesus could probably have functioned quite well in Galilean society with very little Greek language knowledge.

On the Italian peninsula, Latin was the native language. The Romans, however, had such a deep admiration for the Greeks that they made no effort to supplant the Greek language as the Mediterranean *lingua franca* in the first century. In Syro-Palestinian cities with a large number of Roman residents (like Herod's splendid port city, Caesarea), Latin could be heard daily and found in official documents. But generally speaking, very few Latin texts or inscriptions appeared in Palestine in the first century AD.

HELLENISM AND PHYSICAL CULTURE

Physical culture refers to the solid artifacts of a people: what they wore, what they ate, the style of their buildings. In "culture contact" situations (when one group has significant interaction with another) these traits are usually the first ones exchanged. And so it is no surprise that throughout the lands conquered by Alexander and ruled by his successors, we find many artifacts that copy the typical styles of the Greeks. But the influence was not limited to those whom the Greeks conquered. Not long after the time of Alexander, the Romans were exposed to Greek culture from contact with Greek colonies in Italy. By the third century BC, the Romans had largely adopted Greek styles of architecture, clothing, and literature. After Rome had conquered Greece, the influence continued and expanded. Greek slaves were highly prized, and thousands were brought to Rome to serve as personal assistants, advisors, or as tutors for Roman children. The Roman poet Horace (65–8 BC) wrote, "Captive Greece took captive her crude conqueror, and introduced her arts into rude Latium" (*Epistles* II.1). (Unfortunately, as many traditional Romans would lament, she also introduced such vices of hedonism and pederasty.)

The influence of Hellenism throughout the Empire is most obvious in the architectural remains of ancient cities from Ephesus to Egypt. The Greek taste for columns and capitols made its appearance in Judean buildings, including Herod's Temple. In the time of Jesus, the Jews avoided the Greek and Roman-style representational decorations on the buildings: there were no gods or heroes, or even animals, cavorting on the friezes of Herod's palace or the governor's mansion. The Jews of Jesus' day were very suspicious of such decorations, regarding them as a possible violation of the prohibition against graven images. Instead, they adorned their houses and buildings with geometric patterns and plant motifs.

Of course, it was not only the building styles that were influenced by the West. The layouts of cities, too, underwent a change, as a central courtyard replaced the city gates as the place of meeting and judgment. Household furnishings adapted to the times. The eastern custom of sitting on the floor was displaced (in urban areas at least) by the Greek custom of sitting on benches or couches. Free men, when they dined, reclined on couches. Slaves would stand or kneel to serve their masters. Even clothing style was influenced, as the shorter Greek-style robe largely replaced the traditional longer garb of eastern men.

HELLENISTIC ATTITUDES AND PHILOSOPHIES

These changes are all what we might call "cosmetic." There were, however, some more substantial results from the Greek cultural domination. There was, for instance, an obvious change in the status and roles of women. Greek society tended to place very little value on women.

Female babies were routinely abandoned or killed. Adult women were little better than domestic servants. Generally they did not buy or sell property, run businesses, and were not allowed to enter into legal contracts without permission of their *kyrios*, or "lord"—a husband or male relative. This picture is dramatically different from the role of the Proverbs 31 woman of Old Testament Israel, who makes and sells cloth, hires servants, and buys a field without consulting her husband. But by Jesus' day, the Greek attitude toward women had already begun to infiltrate the minds of many Mediterranean peoples, including the Jews (as we shall consider further below).

A more positive influence of Greek thinking can be found in the spread of logical and philosophical methods throughout the Mediterranean world. Philosophy, which emphasizes the use of reason to understand the nature of the universe, germinated in the rocky Greek soil, and it came to full flower at Athens. Plato was the philosopher *par excellence* of the ancient world, and his ideas have influenced many thinkers throughout history. Plato's pupil Aristotle was the tutor of Alexander the Great, and Alexander took scrolls of his teacher's writings with him on his eastern campaign. Once the teachings of the philosophers had been transplanted to Asia, they took root and grew into unique Eastern varieties. Alexandria in Egypt became a major center for philosophical and scientific investigation, encouraged by the great library of world literature established there sometime around 300 BC. In Alexandria, the Jewish scholar Philo forged his own brand of Platonism, a school of philosophy that taught the existence of an ideal spiritual world. And more than a century before Philo's time, the Alexandrian Eratosthenes, using the logical methods of the Greeks, had calculated that the world is a sphere of 24,000 miles circumference (only 800 miles off!) located 92 million miles from the sun (a mere million miles short of the actual distance).

But Alexandria was not the only eastern city that produced scholars. Zeno, the founder of the school of thought known as Stoicism, was evidently from Phoenicia. Epicureanism, another well known ancient philosophy, established schools at Syrian Antioch, as well as Alexandria. And a couple hundred years after Jesus' time, a school of thought called Neo-Platonism, which would have a profound influence on Saint Augustine and Christianity, would originate from the Greco-Egyptian philosopher Plotinus.

Other than Philo and some other Alexandrian Jewish thinkers he mentions, there is little evidence that the Greek philosophy had much of a direct impact on Jewish thought. In the Apocrypha, the pseudepigrapha, and the Dead Sea Scrolls, one searches in vain for evidence that the Palestinian Jews had even a rudimentary familiarity with Greek philosophy. Even in later rabbinic literature, where the rabbis make reference to Homer's writings and acknowledge his high esteem among the Greeks, there is no shred of an indication that they had ever actually read any of his works. Most of the Jews apparently believed that true wisdom was to be found not through reason, but through the divine revelation recorded in the Holy Scriptures.

THE NEAR EASTERN CULTURAL CONTEXT

The Jews of Jesus' day were a Middle Eastern people, a Semitic race closely related to the Idumeans, Moabites, Phoenicians, and Syrians. For many centuries before the time of Jesus, they had lived and interacted with their kin in the rugged region known as the Levant. While we should not undervalue the unique features of Jewish culture, we should expect that these Semitic nations would have a great deal in common. So we would not be disappointed, then, to discover that many of the customs and mores of Jewish society were part of the greater Near Eastern landscape.

For instance, almost all Near Eastern men wore beards, while Greeks and Romans were often clean shaven. Likewise, one would be hard pressed to distinguish the typical clothing of a Jewish peasant from that of a Syrian or Arabian. For the Jewish people, some of the shared customs became sacred law. Circumcision was practiced by the Egyptians, as well as by the Phoenicians, Syrians, and Moabites (among others). Among the Jews, however, this custom had special religious significance, as it was considered the sign of God's covenant with Abraham. The Greeks, and later the Romans, looked on the custom with contempt, since they regarded any mutilation of the body to be scandalous. But their attempts to suppress the practice always met with violent responses from the natives. Yet another example: most of the Semitic peoples (with the exception of the Babylonians and Assyrians) considered the pig to be an unclean animal. Some of the Canaanites and Syrians used it in sacrifices to underworld deities, but it was not considered a fit sacrifice to the main gods, and certainly not for human consumption. Once again, the Jews seem to have been especially scrupulous in this matter, regarding abstention from pork as a holy obligation. Their position puzzled the Greeks and Romans, who considered pork one of the most delicious of meats.

THE NEAR EASTERN MIND

While such customs as these certainly help us to identify the Jewish people with their Near Eastern neighbors, they are in a sense "incidentals"—they do not really capture the most substantial differences between the East and the West. It has been said that the "primitive" people of the East looked at natural phenomenon and asked "Who?," while people of the West asked "How?"[1] This is certainly an oversimplification, but it does contain a grain of truth. There was a pervasive spirituality to Eastern culture that was somewhat diminished in the West. The Greek thinkers would seek naturalistic explanations for why the wind blows or why the river flows downhill, questions few Easterners would concern themselves with. But even if they were shown and understood the Greeks' clever explanations, the Easterners would generally not have been impressed. To the people of the East, these were but mechanisms, and the true explanation for natural phenomena lay in the gods and spirits who commanded the elements.

There was also a greater sense of communal identity in the East. In the West, individuals were becoming increasingly significant. Athletic competitions, gladiatorial games, and chariot races could make men into great celebrities. The East had no such traditions of one-on-one competition. In fact, with the exception of warfare, there were few realms of life in the Near East where an individual could truly distinguish themselves in such a manner. In the time of Jesus, the Greek and Roman worlds were producing great authors, poets, and biographers. Figures like Thucydides, Horace, Aristophanes, and Cicero were highly renowned and inspired many imitators. But in the East, many of the greatest works of art and literature were anonymous. They were considered community property, a tradition that could grow with later additions.

MARRIAGE AND FAMILY

Another realm where East and West differed was in the significance of marriage and family. Both Semites and Greeks considered it extremely important to have a son to carry on the family honor. But in the West,

---

1. Frankfort et. al., *Intellectual Adventure*, 15.

there was a deep-seated revulsion for large families (the idea may have originated in deep antiquity, when the Greeks were in constant danger of starvation because of their poor soil and agricultural practices). Abortion and other methods of birth control were used to limit the number of children in the house. Often, however, these methods were unsuccessful, and unwanted children would suffer a gruesome fate. Baby girls were usually abandoned on the hillsides, where they would die of exposure, or be eaten by animals, or collected and raised for prostitution. Even baby boys might be abandoned, if there were already more than one or two children in the house.

But in the East, such practices were almost unknown, since all children were considered gifts from Heaven. The Greeks living in Egypt were puzzled and even amused by the native Egyptians who would gather their abandoned babies and adopt them as their own children. Even the well attested Eastern practice of infant sacrifice cannot be seen as evidence to the contrary: they sacrificed their children because they considered them the greatest gifts that could be offered, not because they thought them worthless. True, sons were valued more than daughters, but large families with many boys and girls were considered a great blessing (see Job 42:13–15). To that end, wealthy men often had multiple wives. In the Near East, the ability to support many wives was considered a sign of honor. Solomon's wealth was epitomized by the fact that he kept seven hundred wives and three hundred concubines (1 Kgs 11:3). In the West, on the other hand, only one wife was allowed, although almost all wealthy men kept mistresses or young male lovers on the side. The Greek preference for monogamy was not so much a matter of morality as of economy—multiple wives would mean more mouths to feed.

THE JEWISH CULTURAL CONTEXT

We have already observed the somewhat obvious fact that the ancient Jews were people of the Greco-Roman world, and more specifically, one of several Semitic races. But they were also unique in many ways. Of course, there was their religion: no other ethnic group in the ancient world held to belief in only one God. But they also had some unique customs and values—often associated with their religion—that set them apart from their neighbors. For instance, there was apparently a greater resistance to Hellenism among the Jews than was exhibited by some of their neighbors. While the Syrians had little trouble identifying their gods with those of the Greek pantheon, the Jews were unwilling to make such a concession. Furthermore, Greek "secular" activities that had a strong religious component—like athletic competitions or theatrical performances—were viewed with suspicion in Jewish cities. And we have already noted how the Jews rejected Greco-Roman representational art.

But the Jewish people were not about to throw out the baby with the bathwater. The Jews were not opposed to foreign innovations in principle, only in particulars. They had taken easily to the Aramaic language of the Babylonians, embraced the Babylonian calendar, and even found value in some of their religious customs. Three hundred years of Persian domination also made an impression on Judaism, as many ideas of ancient Zoroastrianism (e.g., angel hierarchies, fallen angels, and some notions about the Devil) seemed to enrich the Jews' own faith. The Greeks and Romans, foreign as their ways might be, could also provide some worthwhile new perspectives. Jesus reclined on a bench as he ate the Last Supper, more like a Roman than an ancient Israelite. Herod's building projects employed many of the new engineering techniques developed by the Romans. Caesarea, which became the Roman capital in Palestine, was a showplace for Roman technological ingenuity, and included aqueducts and a modern (for the time) sewage system. Pontius Pilate even built an aqueduct in Jerusalem (although his appropriation of Temple funds for the project nearly provoked a riot). And even though the idea caught on slowly, many Jewish writers found the ideal of monogamy to be very compatible with their faith. In fact, they discovered that the Scriptural story of Adam and Eve seems to implicitly assume monogamy, rather than polygamy.

As we survey briefly some aspects of Jewish culture in this era, we will see both positive and negative effects of Hellenism on Jewish culture. We will also see some remarkable continuity, as many aspects of Jewish life had their roots deep in Old Testament times, but had developed along a natural trajectory into the new age of Roman domination.

BIRTH AND CHILDHOOD

Children were considered the normal and desired outcome of marriage. Methods of birth control were known in the ancient Roman world, but there is no evidence that the Jews used them. Abortion was also practiced, though this procedure was condemned by both Jews and some of their Gentile neighbors. But even after the child was born, there were no guarantees of surviving to adulthood. Some estimate that the infant mortality rate in this era may have been as high as 30%. Given such odds, we might imagine that some parents would have been a little reluctant to become particularly attached to their children, at least until they seemed to have survived the delicate stage of infancy.

The birth would have normally occurred at home. There were not usually doctors to attend to the births, but there were midwives in ancient Judea, skilled in the practice of childbirth. The abilities of these "wise women" were highly respected, and Jewish tradition warned that those who talked back to the midwives risked the lives of their children. They were among the few whom rabbinic tradition allowed to travel and work on the Sabbath day. They were sometimes paid by the recipients of their services, but often the community provided for the support of these important specialists.

As already mentioned, sons were considered more valuable than daughters, but both were precious. Job, after God's blessings had been restored to him, had seven sons and three daughters, an ideal family. Following the birth, the mother was required to undergo a period of ritual washings for purification. During this period, she was not allowed to enter the congregation for worship or to participate in religious ceremonies. Like most ancient Mediterranean peoples, the Jews believed that anyone who experienced discharges of blood or other bodily fluids became "polluted," and this pollution could be transferred to other people or objects, making them unfit to appear before God in worship. So the mother would be unclean and isolated from the community for a week after giving birth to a boy. After the week of separation she was allowed to rejoin community activities, but she could not participate in Temple worship for another thirty-three days. After that period was passed, she would take a bath and bring a special offering to the Temple, to be completely released from her pollution. The periods of purification were doubled if she gave birth to a girl: segregated for two weeks, followed by a sixty-six day period of purification (see Leviticus 12). The shorter period for boys might reflect the greater value attached to boys, but there was also a practical consideration: since the boy had to be circumcised at eight days old, the mother had to be allowed to rejoin the community with her son before the eighth day.

Circumcision, as noted above, was a common custom of several Near Eastern peoples. In Judaism, it was performed when the child was eight days old, as opposed to some other cultures that performed the ritual at puberty. It was more than mere custom, but rather a holy obligation for which the Jews had fought and died. Traditionally, circumcision was performed in the family home. Ideally the father would perform the operation, but Jewish tradition allowed for a specially trained rabbi, known as the *mohel*, to perform the ritual instead. The circumcision was a very important day in the family's life: many relatives and friends would gather to witness the event and feast with the family in celebration. Often, it was also the day when the child was named. Usually, the firstborn son was named after the father or another close male relative.

Children were generally nursed for three years, either by their mother or a wet nurse. As soon as they were weaned, they began to learn their place in the world.

CHILDHOOD AND EDUCATION

In the ancient world, there were few romantic notions attached to childhood. Children were an almost invisible segment of society, seldom seen or heard. They had toys, played games, and made music, but parents and society apparently felt no compulsion to keep children entertained. Childhood was preparation for adulthood, not a time to linger over or dwell upon.

As soon as a child was weaned, they apparently began their education (see Isa 28:13). In the time of Jesus, the principal content of a son's academic education was the Torah, the religious laws (Josephus *Ant.* 4:209–211; Philo *Embassy to Gaius* 31). The pupils may have learned to read and write from the Law, much as the primary grammar book of children in early America was the Bible. If this was the case, then literacy among the ancient Palestinian Jews may have been much more extensive than in surrounding societies, where probably not more than thirty percent of adults could read. But on the other hand, Judaism in this era emphasized memorization and recitation of the Torah, not reading from scrolls, which would have been too expensive for most people to afford anyway.

Most of this training occurred in the home, under the tutelage of the father (see Prov 4:1–9). According to the Talmud (*b. B. Bat.* 21a), a scholar named Joshua ben Gamala was concerned about the inability of many fathers to teach their children properly, so he ordered the establishment of schools in every town and province of Judea and Galilee.

All boys from age six or seven up were sent to the local school to receive their training. The only person we know of by that name from our sources was a high priest who held the office in AD 63–65. By the time of the compilation of the Talmud (fifth-sixth century AD), the existence of schools was considered a given: the *bet hassepher* ("the house of the book") for elementary education, and the *bet hammidrash* ("the house of exposition") for advanced studies in biblical interpretation.

Girls did not attend the schools. Any education they received occurred in the home, and was generally more practical than literary. There were, however, some learned women among the Jews, and ancient manuscripts discovered in the Judean wilderness bear witness to the fact that some Jewish women in the time of Jesus achieved at least a basic level of literacy.

THE HOME

Houses in most ancient Palestinian villages and cities were more like what we would call apartments, or even condominiums. Several living units were joined together in a single building. The doorway opened into a courtyard where there the community well was located. The back wall formed the defensive wall for the village. The typical dwelling was small, consisting of a single multi-purpose room. The walls were usually made of mud bricks, and the floors were made of beaten clay. The roof was flat, usually constructed of thatches laid over a wooden frame and covered with clay. There was often a loft to an upper story of sorts, which served as the sleeping area for the family. Animals might be kept in the lower story in the evening. A brazier provided heat for the household when necessary, though the climate of the region was generally temperate. Cooking, however, was usually done outside.

There was no indoor plumbing for most homes (although modern cities like Caesarea were equipped with public sewer systems). Water was drawn from a common well, and stored in large containers for drinking and other uses. Most Jews did not often use water for bathing, except for ritual purification—washing the hands before meals, or the ritual baths (*mikvah*) required after someone had come into a source of uncleanness. Daily "washing" was usually performed with oil, spread on the skin and then scraped from the body. Water was not used in toilets. Waste was collected in buckets and dumped outside the settlement.

The wealthy were rather better off. Their houses might contain several rooms, and even multiple stories. They were constructed of wooden timbers and cut stone, with tile placed on the floors. A central courtyard might provide fresh air and sunshine during the day. They might be furnished with a fireplace for cooking and heat, and could even have private cisterns and indoor plumbing. The homes of the very rich, like Herod's palaces, were furnished with pools for ritual bathing, toilets that emptied into sewers, and even swimming pools for sport.

DIET

The Jewish people were not big eaters. They generally ate two meals a day (in contrast to the Romans, who ate four). Every meal included bread. The typical bread was made of barley, while the wealthy would enjoy wheat bread. Since there were no preservatives in those days, bread had to be baked often. It was simple fare: flour would be ground in the home, mixed with oil and salt, and perhaps seasoned with honey or other spices.

In addition to bread, meals included a variety of vegetables. Favorites included onions, beans, lentils, or cucumbers. Cheese was also a common part of the diet, made from goats' milk. Eggs were also a good source of protein. Meat was used sparingly, except by those people living near the Sea of Galilee who had an abundant supply of fish. Fowl (usually pigeon, quail, or geese—chickens were still rare in Palestine in Jesus' day) and sometimes lamb were considered a treat. Locusts also were a fairly common commodity. The proverbial "fatted calf," on the other hand, was an indulgence of the rich. Wine was consumed with every meal, even by children, though it was often diluted with water.

MAKING A LIVING

Most Jews in Jesus' day—like the majority of the people throughout the Mediterranean world—made a meager living by subsistence farming. The household was the primary center of the family economy. It was where most food and raw materials were produced and where the raw materials were made into household necessities. Fiber was spun into thread; thread was made into cloth; cloth was sewn into clothes. Most families owned a few goats, geese, or the occasional chicken. Rural families might have donkeys or other plow animals to help with the tilling of fields and taking surplus produce to market. The markets were important town centers, where people could supplement the goods they produced with those produced by their neighbors or imported by merchants. But most people had little money for extravagances or luxuries. They would buy mostly the necessities that they could not produce on their own, like tools, or small indulgences like spices.

Urbanization did increase the opportunities for specialization: you would not have to produce everything you needed if your neighbor produced more than he needed for his own family. So by the time of Jesus, towns and villages were places where people could become skilled workers in their particular specialties. Rabbinic sources and other texts reveal the vast diversity of middle-class occupations: there were scribes, lawyers, teachers, shop keepers, bankers, tax collectors, masons, carpenters, coopers, smiths, tanners and leather-workers, foremen, and fishermen, among others. Jesus is called a "carpenter" (*tekton*) in Mark 6:3. This Greek word could refer to a worker in wood or stone, but ancient translations and other early traditions indicate that a woodworker, especially a furniture maker, was most likely intended here. Although later Roman writers considered Jesus' profession menial, it surely required a greater level of skill than a common laborer would have possessed.

MARRIAGE CUSTOMS

Once a man had the skills or land to make a decent living, he was ready to take a wife. The Mishnah recommends that a man marry when he is eighteen, but that guideline was probably idealistic (*Abot.* 5:21). Many men would not have had the means to support a wife until they were well into their twenties or thirties. Perhaps when he was eighteen, he might be able to choose a wife; but on the other hand, his parents may have already taken care of that task years before, having negotiated the marriage when their son was but a boy. There was a general assumption that a normal Jewish man would be married and fulfilling his God-given duty of carrying on the family. Perpetual bachelorhood was virtually unheard of in the ancient world, except among the Essenes or other religious sects who considered the presence of women a hindrance to godliness.

The rabbis debated extensively the age when a girl was marriageable, and we should probably assume that much of their talk was purely theoretical (it seems quite doubtful that anyone would seriously have assumed that a three year old child could be sexually mature, as the rabbis occasionally argued). Practically speaking, however, girls were considered eligible for marriage as soon as they had reached puberty. Once the negotiations were completed and a contract had been signed, the couple was considered betrothed. Legally, this arrangement was as binding as the marriage itself. The couple was expected to have sexual relations with no one but their betrothed until their wedding (a requirement more stringently enforced in the case of the bride-to-be than the future groom). When the husband had the financial means to support his wife and family, he would make arrangements to claim his wife, bring her into his home and consummate the marriage. Rabbinic traditions allowed the bride and groom to take a year or more to prepare for marriage after the betrothal had been formalized (*m. Ketub.* 5:2).

In Old Testament times, the groom had to demonstrate his financial fitness by paying a *mohar*, or "bride price," to his father-in-law (see Gen 34:12; 1 Sam 18:20–25). But by the time of Jesus, this practice had been modified: the "bride price" had become a deposit that the groom provided, kept in trust by the bride. In the event that the couple was to divorce, this money would be given to the ex-wife. It was essentially the ancient equivalent of a prenuptial agreement, designed to discourage husbands from thoughtlessly dumping their displeasing wives. In New Testament times, the ancient practice of the bride-price was being displaced by the Greek-style dowry, in which the bride's family gave the woman money that she brought with her into the marriage. The larger her dowry, of course, the more likely the young lady would be to find an attractive husband.

There was no "wedding ceremony" *per se* in early Palestinian Jewish society. Marriage was much more a legal arrangement than a religious one. It was the signing of the marriage contract that bound the couple together, and the sexual union that sealed the arrangement. Nonetheless, the time when the husband actually took possession of the bride could be a spectacular affair. According to rabbinic tradition, the groom, dressed in special wedding garments, could proceed through town accompanied by his companions to the bride's house. He would take his bride, accompanied by her attendants, to his own house, where they would celebrate the wedding feast. The feasting could last several days. Finally, the bride and groom would proceed to a special chamber (*kuppa*) where the marriage was consummated.

In the time of Jesus, polygamy (multiple wives) was not unknown, but it was becoming rare. The Old Testament never actually forbids polygamy, even though it does not especially condone the practice, either. Josephus allowed also that Jewish custom permitted a man to have multiple wives (*Ant.* 17:14). Rabbinic tradition allowed a man to have up to five wives if he could afford it, while kings were permitted to have as many as eighteen (*m. Ketub.* 10:5). Practically, however, polygamy was going out of style in Jesus' day. Partly this was due to Greek influence; but it is also clear that the Greek custom of monogamy seemed very compatible with a theological understanding of marriage based on the creation accounts in Genesis.

Divorce was permitted and common in Jewish society. The Old Testament permitted divorce (Deut 24:1), but it was not especially clear on what constituted grounds for divorce. The rabbinic school of Shammai held that immorality was the only appropriate basis for divorce, but the more liberal school of Hillel held that a husband could divorce his wife even for so minor a foible as burning his dinner (*m. Git.* 9:10). The marriage contracts in this period were generally designed with provisions that made it costly for the husband to divorce his wife frivolously. While neither the Bible nor the Mishnah entertained the idea of a wife divorcing her husband, Jewish documents discovered at Aswan in Egypt (the Elephantine Papyri, fifth century BC) and the Talmud assume that a woman possessed that right.

HEALTH AND MEDICINE

Ancient people were subject to a different set of diseases than those that afflict modern Westerners today. Diseases like heart disease and diabetes often are the result of overeating and sedentary lifestyles. Most people of the ancient world did not need to worry much about overeating. And the work involved in making the daily bread was strenuous enough to burn off the calories they consumed from eating it.

Diseases are not described with clinical accuracy in the Bible or other ancient texts, and it is not easy to determine the conditions that the authors are describing. The term "plague" (Hebrew *nega'* or *deber*; Greek *plege*) is used in the Bible for any widespread contagion, including epidemic diseases like the bubonic plague or the Black Death. The rabbis defined a plague more specifically as a disease that kills 500 able-bodied men in three days (*m. Ta'an.* 3:4). Such plagues could destroy entire populations, and seemed to defy any treatment. Consumption—"wasting disease"—was also a dreaded killer. This term could refer to tuberculosis, but it might also mean parasitic infections such as malaria, typhoid fever, or dysentery that made it impossible for their victims to keep down food or water. Such plagues were often, but not always, considered a judgment from God. Cancer, too, was well known in the ancient world. It was first described in Egyptian texts dating from 1500 BC, and various methods were indicated for its treatment. The Greek Hippocrates (460–377 BC) made a study of the disease and coined the term "cancer." But there was no special term for cancer in the Bible.

Ancient people were also afflicted with many non-fatal conditions. Diseases of the eyes were a common complaint. Cataracts could render one completely blind and practically helpless in ancient Israel. In the Apocrypha, Tobit was blinded by cataracts contracted after bird droppings fell into his eyes (Tob 2:10). A more common cause of blindness was trachoma, a disease that could be transmitted by flies or by contact with infected bodily fluids. Also, epilepsy-like symptoms are described in numerous ancient texts, including the Gospels (Matt 17:15; Mark 9:17–18; Luke 9:39). Many ancient peoples considered this disease a sign of divine visitation, and would often encourage seizures as a path to prophetic revelation. In the Gospels, however, epileptic symptoms are attributed to demonic activity.

One of the most stigmatized conditions of the ancient world was what most Bible translations inaccurately call "leprosy." There is little evidence that Hansen's Disease, the contagious and largely incurable disfiguring malady that we call leprosy, was common in Israel. Rather, the Old Testament uses the word *tsara'at* for a variety of skin conditions, and in the New Testament, the Greek word *lepra* should probably be understood in the same broad manner. The Bible mentions such symptoms as flaking and peeling skin, reddening and thickening of the tissues, blisters, and dry white patches, suggesting diseases such as psoriasis, dermatitis, or fungal infections. Such skin conditions are common in poor agrarian societies, often arising from bad diet and inadequate hygiene. In Jewish culture, such unsightly conditions rendered a person ritually unclean, unable to take part in worship. Since anyone who came in contact with the "lepers" was rendered temporarily unclean, they were often segregated from society.

For the most part, ancient people were unaware of what caused diseases. The Greeks developed mistaken theories about imbalances of bodily fluids, but the Jews seem to have avoided speculating on the topic at all. The Bible and other Jewish writers (including Josephus and Philo of Alexandria) attribute some diseases to angels or demons, but they were also well aware that diseases could have natural causes. Jesus, for instance, plainly says that "The sick need a physician" (Matt 9:12), not that they need an exorcist. In cases of natural illness, medicines or even surgery were believed to be in order. In Old Testament times, there was a good deal of suspicion about the doctors' skills (see Job 13:4; Jer 8:22–9:6), but their reputation seems to have improved a little by New Testament times. Josephus attributes to the Essenes (see Chapter 7) the ability to cure illnesses by their herbal arts (*War* 2:136). Generally in the ancient world, the Greeks were considered especially able physicians, and Greek slaves were often sought and trained to be personal physicians to the wealthy.

DEATH AND BURIAL

"The length of our years is seventy; or if vigorous, eighty..." (Psa 90:10). The Psalmist believed a person could expect to live seventy years, or even eighty. And yet, in the time of Jesus, such long lifespans seem to have been the exception rather than the rule. Certainly, many of the wealthy and comfortable managed to go to their graves "full of years." But among the poor—which constituted the bulk of society—an elderly person was an oddity. The average lifespan in Rome in the first century AD seems to have been about thirty. Overcrowding facilitated the spread of disease, and malnutrition made it difficult to fight off its effects. Furthermore, many women died in childbirth, bringing down the average life expectancy even more. In lands like Judea where the population was more dispersed, the situation was a little better. But even here, the average life expectancy was only about fifty years.

Death was generally not a welcome prospect in ancient Judea. Even people with a sincere hope of resurrection did not blithely accept the idea of earthly existence coming to an end. But in a world where death could strike any household at any age, it was impossible for people to deny their mortality, like we sometimes do today. Life proceeded with the nagging awareness that death was ever imminent, and no one's tomorrows were guaranteed.

While we might imagine that this awareness would make people more stoical about death, there is no evidence that this was the case. It was expected that the passing of a loved one would be met with dramatic displays. People would wail and weep, throwing themselves on the body. They would tear their clothes, dress in sackcloth, and cover themselves with dust or ashes. Sometimes, they would even tear out their own hair by the handfuls. Professional mourners were hired to add to the demonstration. The presence of these paid participants was not considered hypocritical. Indeed, it was considered an important way of honoring the dead. The Mishnah commanded that even the poorest man should hire at least one wailing woman and a couple musicians at the passing of his wife (*m. Ketub.* 4:4). Their short and fragile lives were considered no less precious than our longer lives.

Bodies of the dead were washed and could be wrapped in linen burial shrouds. Washing was considered so important that the rabbis even permitted it to be done on the Sabbath (*m. Shabb.* 23:5). It was common for spices like myrrh and frankincense to be placed with the body (see 2 Chron 16:14), or even in the folds of the burial shroud. Such a practice was used in Egypt for the preservation of the corpse, but the Jews had no particular interest in mummification. Rather, the spices were simply used to honor the dead and enhance the enjoyment of those who might visit the tomb.

In Jewish law, contact with dead bodies was considered defiling, rendering a person ritually unclean for worship. The Jews did not practice cremation except as a form of punishment, so it was important that dead bodies be dealt with properly or the land would become defiled. Cemeteries were therefore considered unclean places, and were always located apart from human habitations, often just outside the city walls. (Those who had been executed were usually laid in a special cemetery even farther out of town, but this was custom, not law.) Most of the dead were simply buried in the ground, but people with the means often purchased a plot in a tomb. The tombs were dug out in the sides of cliffs, sometimes adapted from old quarries. On the paths that led to the tombs, trees and shrubs were often planted, creating a peaceful garden-like setting. They were frequently decorated with rich facades. The tombs were generally constructed with two chambers: a shallow antechamber inside the entrance, divided by a partial wall from the inner burial chamber. The entrance to the burial chamber was quite small, requiring anyone to stoop in order to enter. Inside the burial chamber, shelves were hewn out of the rock where the bodies were laid. Often, these tombs were "family plots," containing the remains of all the members of the clan. Sometimes, the dead were buried in wooden coffins that could be painted with elaborate designs. The bodies were placed in these coffins facing upward, often with some personal items placed at their head or feet.

In the time of Jesus, the Jews adopted for a while the somewhat strange custom called "secondary burial." The deceased were placed in a tomb until the flesh had decayed, and then the bones were gathered and placed in a special box called an "ossuary." Usually, these boxes were cut from a block of limestone and were rectangular, measuring about two feet long by one foot wide and deep. They were frequently decorated with geometric or plant motifs. The deceased's name was scratched or inscribed on the box, often in informal script. Various personal effects were sometimes left near the boxes. It was a typical custom in the ancient world to leave precious items in the tombs so the deceased could use them in the next life, but this does not seem to be the motivation for the Jewish tomb deposits. Perhaps they were merely following the convention of the day, without ascribing to it any supernatural significance.

The practice of secondary burial continued in Judea from about 20 BC to AD 70. After that time, the procedure was mostly abandoned, and the upper-class Jews returned to the earlier practice of placing the dead in a coffin laid in a communal tomb.

7

Jesus' Religious Context

THE RELIGIOUS WORLD IN which Jesus lived was fully as diverse as the world in which we live today. There was the official religious establishment, based in the Jerusalem temple. There were several major Jewish "denominations," each generally regarded as an authentic expression of Jewish piety, and yet deeply divided by their beliefs and practices. There were many small splinter groups, and many Jewish people who did not align themselves with any particular group or movement. There were religious communes in various locales, each with its own set of rules and requirements. There were itinerant teachers with their bands of disciples. And then, there were the "others": the Gentiles (non-Jews) who often lived in close proximity to the Jewish majority, worshipping their various gods in private shrines or public temples, and expressing their allegiance to the Empire through the veneration of the Emperor and the spirit of Rome.

Jesus' ministry to the "lost sheep of Israel" (Matt 15:24) rarely brought him into conflict with pagan religious beliefs or practices. In fact, as noted earlier, the population of Galilee was overwhelmingly Jewish. Since Jesus probably had little contact with Gentiles, we shall devote only a brief discussion to the Jews' pagan neighbors. On the other hand, Jesus was constantly butting heads against various Jewish religious leaders, and it was partly this conflict that led to his crucifixion. A general understanding of Jewish religious beliefs and practices in first-century Palestine is essential for a real comprehension of Jesus' ministry.

PAGANS IN PALESTINE

In Old Testament times, Israel was surrounded by indigenous Canaanites who worshipped (among other deities) the storm god Baal and the fertility goddess Asherah. But with the coming of the Greeks, there was a major cultural upheaval in Palestine. There was an influx of foreigners—Greeks and Macedonians—who brought their own particular beliefs with them. Usually, these beliefs involved the worship of the gods of Greek mythology. Their chief god was Zeus, the storm god, who ruled over a pantheon of thirteen major gods and a host of minor deities. They included such formidable figures as Poseidon, god of the seas; Hades, the lord of the underworld; and Aphrodite, the goddess of love. There were gods and goddesses of rivers, of winds, and even of wine. The average Gentile could be kept very busy attempting to appease the different deities, or very entertained attending the festivals of various gods.

Most of the Greeks, and even the Romans, shared some basic ideas about the identities and attributes of the chief deities. But beyond some general tenets, there was no shared set of beliefs that can be called "the Greek religion." There was a great body of conflicting traditions and rituals regarding the gods, and there was no central authority that could pronounce which versions of the stories were true and which were false. In the various cities and regions of the Mediterranean world, cults of the gods took very different forms. For instance, the fertility goddess worshipped as "Diana" in Asia Minor bore little resemblance to the virgin goddess of the hunt honored by the same name in Greece. Yet, the contradictions do not seem to have been a cause of major concern. As far as we know, there were no efforts to stamp out heresies and impose a standard form of religion throughout Greco-Roman society.

Many of the gods and goddesses had special relationships with particular cities or locations. For example, Athena was the patron goddess of Athens, as Diana was the principal goddess of Ephesus. These cities would devote a great deal of money and energy to the temples and priests (or priestesses) of their gods, and their shrines would become centers of pilgrimage. On the other hand, some gods were more widely honored than others (Dionysus, the god of wine, seemed to enjoy a good deal of popularity). Individuals might profess a special devotion to their local god, yet enthusiastically participate in the feasts or rites of other deities.

With the Seleucid Empire encouraging the spread of Greek culture, there was a tendency in Palestine toward "syncretism"—the combination of religions into one. Among the natives, this trend manifested itself in the identification of Greek gods with native deities. Baal and Zeus were both storm gods, and so it was no great leap for native Semites to worship Baal under the name Zeus Ouranos—Zeus of the Heavens. This practice was especially popular with the native social climbers who sought to curry the favor of their overlords by imitating their ways and beliefs. But on the other hand, it is almost certain that many native peoples resisted this trend, preferring their traditional ways to those of the newcomers. It is unfortunate that the practices of the "common people" rarely leave a mark in the archeological record.

It is important to note that not everyone was a devotee of the old deities. There was also a growing class of people in the ancient Mediterranean world that was quite skeptical about the ancient myths. The philosophically inclined might find their spiritual expression in such schools of thought as Stoicism or Platonism. These movements provided a sense of purpose and moral instructions that a purely secular life could not. There were also many Greeks and Romans who were finding their way into various Eastern religions, or religions that blended elements of both East and West. Some of the so-called "mystery cults" (so called because of their private initiations and secret rites) fall into this category, as does that ill-defined complex of beliefs that would become known as "Gnosticism" in the second century AD.

THE ROYAL CULT

An important aspect of Greek religion, later adopted by the Romans, was the cult of the ruler. Even before the time of Alexander the Great, the Greeks had begun to deify some of their dead kings (perhaps in imitation of the Egyptians). Alexander the Great was honored as a god in Egypt while he was still living—a tradition derived from the worship of the ancient pharaohs. Later, Alexander's successors claimed to be divine, and cults were established in their honor throughout the Near East. The Egyptians participated in these cults alongside Greeks and Macedonians, but the Jews and other Near Eastern peoples held aloof, at least initially. While Middle Eastern traditions had included the veneration of kings, the worship of living monarchs as gods was apparently unknown in the East outside of Egypt.

The coming of the Romans had little immediate impact on this situation. The Romans made no efforts to impose their own versions of the classical pantheon on the people they conquered. But by the time of Christ, a new "player" had emerged on the religious scene, one that would one day become very significant for both Jews and Christians: the Roman state cult. The state cult apparently originated spontaneously among the Greeks, who attached to their Roman overlords the same divine cachet that they had accorded the Greek monarchs. The ever-practical Roman rulers saw the value of having a single religion unifying the whole empire. They first tolerated, then encouraged, and finally required the Roman subjects to participate in the state religion.

The demands of the religion were not strenuous. Shrines were established throughout the empire where the goddess Roma, who epitomized the spirit of Rome, was given her dues. Also, it was believed that deceased emperors had been welcomed into the divine pantheon of gods, and prayers and sacrifices were offered to Augustus and other dead kings. Occasionally, even a living monarch (Caligula and Nero) claimed to be divine and deserving of worship. Up to the time of Jesus, however, this cult had little direct impact on Palestinian Judaism. Because of the friendship between Herod the Great and Julius Caesar, Judaism was given the privileged position of a "protected religion" in the Roman Empire. The Jews were not forced to participate in the state cult. Instead, they performed sacrifices in of the Jerusalem Temple each day for the well being of the Emperor. Still, the refusal of the Jews to participate in the state cult won them no friends. It reinforced the image that many Greco-Roman people had of the Jewish people as "haters of humanity," a peculiar and anti-social race.

THE "ALMOST JEWS"

It is not always easy to divide everyone in the Roman Empire into the categories of "Jew" or "pagan." There were some troubling people in the middle, people who were good and moral, and even worshipped the God of Abraham, Isaac, and Jacob, and yet, were still on the "outside."

The most well known of these people were the Samaritans. The term "Samaritan" derives from the name of the capital of the old northern Israelite kingdom, Samaria. According to 2 Kings 17, the Samaritans were descendants of people from various nations whom the Assyrians had brought in to resettle Israel after they had deported the original inhabitants. But their worship of pagan gods in his land provoked the Lord to send lions against these new residents. Therefore, the king of Assyria sent an Israelite priest to teach the Samaritans about the God of the land in which they dwelt. They established a temple for his worship on Mount Gerizim in Samaria, and adopted many of the trappings of the Yahwistic faith. The Lord thus became the chief God of Samaria, though the Old Testament maintains that the Samaritans continued to worship other gods, as well.

The Jews and Samaritans had rocky relations through the years. In the days of Zerubbabel (ca. 520 BC), the Samaritans offered to help the people of Judah rebuild the Jerusalem temple, but they were rudely rebuffed (Ezra 4:1–5). Afterwards, the Samaritans attempted to block the project through both political channels and through sabotage (4:6–24). A little later, the Samaritan leaders conspired to stop Nehemiah from rebuilding the walls of Jerusalem (Nehemiah 4). After Alexander the Great conquered the east in 332 BC, the Samaritans rebelled against their new overlord. Alexander responded ruthlessly, and the Jews may well have had a hand in the Samaritans' humiliation. Still later, sometime around 128 BC, the Jewish ruler John Hyrcanus destroyed the temple on Mount Gerizim, and about 107 BC he destroyed the Samaritan city of Shechem. It is no wonder that by the time of Jesus, the "Jews have no dealings with Samaritans" (John 4:9)!

In spite of this history of animosity, the Jews and Samaritans actually shared many characteristics. Both worshiped the Lord, and used the Pentateuch (the first five books of the Old Testament) as their primary Scriptures. The semi-paganism of the Samaritans so despised in the Old Testament seems to have disappeared by the time of Jesus, and the Jewish rabbis observed that the Samaritans were often more scrupulous about keeping the Law than they were themselves (*b. Hul.* 4a). But there were still substantial differences between the groups: the Samaritans' Pentateuch differed in some substantial ways from that of the Jews. They also denied the authority of the biblical historical books, the Prophets, and the poetic and wisdom books.

But the most important difference between the Jews and the Samaritans was that the Samaritans denied the legitimacy of the Jerusalem Temple. Instead, they continued to offer their sacrifices at a shrine on Mt. Gerizim, near the city of Shechem. Some differences of practice and opinion could well have been overlooked by the Jews. But reverence of the Jerusalem Temple, as we shall discuss below, was considered a non-negotiable of Jewish identity.

Other "almost Jews" included those Gentiles who found the morals and beliefs of Judaism attractive, but not attractive enough to get them to convert. In the Bible, they are called "God fearers" (e.g., Acts 13:16). They would send gifts to the Jewish temple, read the Jewish Scriptures, refrain from work on the Sabbath, and perhaps eat kosher foods. They might even attend synagogue services, even though they were typically only permitted to sit in the gallery. But they remained on the periphery of the Jewish nation, since the men were (understandably) reluctant to undergo the ritual of circumcision required for conversion to Judaism. Besides, Jewish tradition held that such righteous Gentiles had a place in Heaven. Actual conversion probably seemed an unnecessary imposition. These God-fearers had to make significant sacrifices for their fascination with Judaism even without converting. Greek and Roman orators and playwrights often castigated or satirized their countrymen who found the Jewish way of life attractive.

THE TRUE JEWS

The most basic of these distinctive features, in a world where most people believed in a multitude of divinities, was the belief in a single, all-powerful God. A proselyte would trade a pantheon of powers for a sole sovereign Lord; there could be no negotiation on this point. Native born Jews would have had the uniqueness of their God drilled into their minds since birth, as many Jewish homes began and ended their day with the recitation of the central affirmation of Judaism, the Shema`: "Hear, O Israel, the Lord is our God, the Lord alone" (Deut 6:4). This verse asserted not only the unique existence of the Lord, but also his special relationship with the Israelites. They were the "chosen people," the ones to whom God had revealed himself, and the ones through whom he would reveal himself to the nations of the world.

THE SCRIPTURES

Israel's unique relationship with God was most clearly manifested in the great gift he had entrusted to the Jews: the written Scriptures. The belief in the authority of the canonical Scriptures—a collection of texts that was considered a uniquely inspired record of God's words for his people—was one of the most remarkable characteristics of the Jewish people. For modern Christians, this idea might seem rather obvious. But in the ancient world, the concept was totally unique. It is true that there were other religions that had books that were regarded as divinely inspired. The Greeks believed that the writings of Homer revealed deep truths to those who were able to interpret them properly. Hesiod was regarded as an inspired author in some Greek circles. But there is no parallel to the Jewish idea of a well defined collection of authoritative religious texts—a "canon"—that shaped the faith and the daily lives of its readers.

Most scholars would agree that beginning in the time of Ezra (in the fifth century BC), the books associated with Moses achieved an unprecedented prominence in Judaism. As the governor of Judah, Ezra had been given authority by the Persian Empire to make the Jewish people live according to "the laws of [their] God" (Ezra 7:11–26). For Ezra, this meant the laws of Moses, which he had made the object of his lifelong study (Ezra 7:6). He instituted public readings of the Scripture and used his position as governor to impose the observance of the law on the Jewish people. So from Ezra's time on, Judaism was in the process of becoming the first "religion of the Book"—a faith centered on accepted Scriptures.

Sometime after the "canonization" (official recognition) of the Books of Moses, the historical and prophetic books, already regarded as divinely inspired and authoritative, were collected and added to the canon. Finally, a third collection of poetic and wisdom texts (e.g., Psalms, Job, Proverbs) was assembled, and granted by general consensus the status of authoritative Scripture. According to rabbinic tradition, the contents of the Jewish canon were officially endorsed by a meeting of rabbis at the town of Jamnia in AD 90. While many scholars have questioned the validity of this tradition, it cannot be denied that Josephus, writing at the end of the first century AD, considered the Jewish canon to be fixed and unalterable (*Against Apion* 1:37–42). It seems likely that the Jewish people widely recognized a select body of books as authoritative, but practically speaking, it was not until the rabbinic era (fourth century AD forward) that there existed an official body that could pronounce an authoritative judgment on this or other religious matters.

The process leading to the closing of the canon was not an altogether smooth one. There was some lingering debate about which books should be included. The group responsible for collecting the Dead Sea Scrolls probably rejected the validity of the Book of Esther. Being radically opposed to the idea of intermarriage with Gentiles, the Scrolls sect probably found Esther's method of saving her people by marrying a Persian king difficult to endorse. In rabbinic literature of the second and third centuries AD, there are records of debates about the canonicity of

Ecclesiastes and the Song of Solomon. The secular nature of these texts was offensive to some of the rabbis. There is even reason to believe that the Sadducees, like the Samaritans, accepted only the books of Moses (the Pentateuch) as authoritative Scripture. Nonetheless, there could be no argument about the validity and importance of a received body of Scripture, at least consisting of the Books of Moses.

DISTINCTIVE JEWISH PRACTICES

The laws of Moses bound the Jews to some practices that made them conspicuous in the ancient world. First, there was circumcision. As mentioned earlier, circumcision was not a uniquely Jewish custom, being practiced by a number of Near Eastern peoples, including the Arabs and the Egyptians. But the Jews attached a unique religious meaning to the custom, holding it to be the sign of the covenant established between God and Abraham (Genesis 17). But among the Greeks and those who adopted their ways, any such defacements of the body's natural appearance were considered abhorrent. Jews who wanted to fit in with Greek culture found ways to "undo" their circumcision—at least cosmetically (1 Macc 1:15). Likewise, the Jews' refusal to eat "unclean" animals, especially pigs, was widely regarded as ridiculous. The Greeks were very fond of pork, and the idea that the Jews' God had forbidden them to partake of such a rich pleasure was incomprehensible to them. Finally, there was nothing in the ancient world that compared to the Jews' Sabbath observance. On the last day of the week, the Jews refused to engage in any kind of work or commerce. Not even slaves could be persuaded to violate the sanctity of this weekly holiday. Roman leaders, perplexed by the significance that the Jewish people throughout the Empire attached to this day, tried to explain it away as an excuse for laziness. But the simple dignity of the Sabbath made a deep impression on the "God fearers" of the Gentile lands, and (much to the chagrin of satirists and politicians) not a few Greeks and Romans began to imitate the Jewish Sabbath observance.

These distinctive practices made the Jews appear eccentric—perhaps even odious—to their Gentile neighbors. But none of them alone was sufficient to identify someone as a Jew. Samaritans obeyed the laws of Moses; Arabs practiced circumcision; God fearers might abstain from pork. So what was the true mark of a Jew? Apparently, the most important criterion was one's attitude toward the Jerusalem temple establishment.

Since the time of King Josiah's religious reforms (622 BC), the Temple in Jerusalem had been the only truly legitimate site for Jewish sacrificial worship. Not that there were no other Jewish temples in the world. We know that in the intertestamental period, there were a couple Jewish temples in Egypt, and another was later established in Jordan. But these temples were constructed with their doors facing Jerusalem—a constant reminder that the true House of the Lord was located in God's holy city. This issue of temple location, as the woman at the well correctly recognized (John 4:20), was the real point of contention between the Jews and the Samaritans. It would also be a major cause of division between Judaism and Christianity. After the destruction of Herod's Temple, Christians would argue that the Temple's fall was an obvious sign that the age of sacrifice was passed, and Judaism itself had become obsolete. It was an argument that struck at the very heart of Jewish identity, and made fellowship between the groups very difficult.

THE TEMPLE IN JEWISH WORSHIP

The Jerusalem Temple had both religious and civil significance for the Jewish people. Its civil significance, discussed earlier, included its roles as a repository of wealth and as a source of national pride. In this chapter, we will focus on the Temple as a center of Jewish religious life.

The Jewish people could hardly imagine religion apart from the Temple. Since the time of Moses, there had been a central shrine where the Hebrews had performed their sacrifices, offered their prayers, and expressed their hopes. The original tabernacle, constructed to house the Ark of the Covenant, had served this function for the early Israelites. Around 950 BC, Solomon's Temple replaced the tabernacle as the principal religious site of Israel. Located on an elevated plateau overlooking the Kidron Valley (the Temple Mount), it became the center of pilgrimage for all the Israelites. After the reforming work of King Josiah, Solomon's Temple was designated as the only legitimate place for the sacrifices that took away the nation's sin. (Prior to Josiah, the Temple had been the chief shrine, but other local shrines had existed, as well.) When the Babylonians destroyed the Temple in 587 BC, the Jewish people were forced to reassess its significance somewhat. No doubt it was during this time that the emphasis on Scripture-centered piety first appeared. But there was never any question of whether or not the Temple would be rebuilt; it was only a matter of when. When it was completed in 515 BC, the Second Temple immediately assumed the role that Solomon's edifice had occupied as the focus of Judah's piety, and of its pride.

Pride was a sore spot for many years. During the Persian period (538–332 BC), Judah did not have the resources to build the kind of glorious structure that would befit the God of the Universe. Still, the Temple was not wanting for its benefactors: wealthy Jews scattered around the Mediterranean world, as well as foreign well-wishers, lavished gifts on the house of Israel's God. During the reign of the Hasmoneans (ca. 140–63 BC), there ensued an era of prosperity and expansion that once again benefited the Temple complex. But it was the "half-Jew" Herod the Great who truly devoted himself to glorifying the Jerusalem Temple complex. Around 20 BC, he announced his plans to expand the Jerusalem Temple dramatically. His vision was as great as his insecurity. He dreamed of creating a temple complex that would be the envy of the entire Roman Empire—and he succeeded. The Temple Mount itself was not large enough to contain Herod's ambitions, and so he had a retaining wall built on the mountain top, and a new plateau constructed. The man-made mesa covered more than thirty acres. As mentioned earlier, Jewish priests were employed and trained to carry out the actual construction work, so that the sanctity of the project would not be compromised. Since the priests insisted that the daily sacrifices could not be interrupted during the entire construction project, Herod was forced to build his new temple literally around the old temple.

The new building was a wonder of the ancient world. It remains, to this day, the largest temple compound ever constructed. The entire complex was surrounded by a massive wall, and there were eight gates that allowed entrance. The Temple compound was divided into a series of courts, restricting access to the holier precincts. Everyone was permitted to ascend into the outer area, the Court of the Gentiles, where sightseers could admire Herod's impressive architecture. This court served as a bazaar, where Roman money could be exchanged for a special "temple currency" that did not bear the Emperor's image, and where sacrificial animals could be purchased. It was separated by another wall from the Court of Women, which only Jews could enter. Signs posted above the gates in this partition warned that any Gentiles entering the Court of the Women would be put to death. But there was a place here for any Jews who wanted to join together in worship, singing, dancing, and celebration—but not sacrifices. The sacrifices could only be witnessed from the next court, the Court of Israelites. This court was actually a narrow strip about sixteen feet wide. Only Jewish men who were ritually clean could enter here, where they had a clear view of the priests conducting their rituals. From this court, the temple personnel ascended a couple stairs and passed through a low embankment to enter the Court of Priests. It was here that most of the daily rituals and regular sacrifices occurred. Beyond the Court of the Priests, there was the Temple building itself. Within these walls were housed the sacred vessels: the lamp stand, the incense altar, the table for the "Bread of the Presence." A thick curtain covered the entrance to the Most Holy Place (the "Holy of Holies"), which was merely an empty chamber—the Ark of the Covenant that was supposed to occupy that place had been lost long centuries earlier, during the Babylonian Exile.

An astounding variety of sacrifices occurred in the Temple precincts. Sometimes, Christians have the impression that all sacrifices were designed to take away sins. But in fact, the majority of sacrifices had nothing to do with the forgiveness of sin. Each morning, the priests would perform the *tamid*, or perpetual daily sacrifice, as an act of divine adoration. There was also a daily sacrifice offered for the health and well-being of the Empire. Furthermore, worshippers could bring sacrificial animals to Jerusalem as thanksgiving or fellowship offerings whenever they desired, as a sign of their devotion to God. There were also purification offerings, performed by those who had contracted some kind of ritual uncleanness. Bodily discharges (such as blood), contact with unclean animals, or touching dead bodies were all deemed "defiling," rendering one unfit for participation in worship until the impurity was removed by ritual washing and the offering of sacrifices. There were sacrifices offered on behalf of one's firstborn child as a sign that the child had been "redeemed" from the Lord, who claimed all firstborn offspring (Exod 13:12-13; Num 18:15). In addition, the Temple received many sacrifices from Gentiles, simply designed to honor the God of Israel.

Sacrifices could take many forms—animals, grains, or monetary gifts. But when someone needed to atone for their sins, they were required to offer an animal sacrifice. Sin offerings could be offered at any time in the Temple, and undoubtedly accounted for a lot of the priests' work. But the highlight of the priests' activities occurred on that one day when they performed the ritual that atoned for the intentional and unintentional transgressions of the entire nation—the Day of Atonement

(Leviticus 16). This annual ceremony centered on the person of the high priest, who transferred the collective sins of Israel to a goat that was driven out into the wilderness. In Jesus' time, there was a complex order to the ceremony which involved numerous washings, changes of clothing, and auxiliary sacrifices. It was the climax of the entire year, the day when the priests "earned their keep." In the minds of many Jews, the ritual of the Day of Atonement was critical for the continuation of their nation. If the collective guilt of the nation were not eradicated, the land was in danger of falling under the curse of God's disfavor.

It should be mentioned here that sacrifice was considered the primary way of dealing with the guilt of sin, but it was not the sole method. Many Jewish texts of the intertestamental era continued to espouse the old prophetic understanding that works of righteousness and charity were more efficacious for forgiveness than any sacrificial offerings (see Mark 12:28–34). In the Dead Sea Scrolls, we find the idea that the prayers of righteous individuals could atone for the sins of the nation. Several texts seem to imply that the suffering of the righteous, too, could help to preserve the nation from the penalties of its iniquity. But few Jews would have denied that sacrifices, properly offered, would turn away God's wrath from his people.

THE PRIESTHOOD

As the agents of atonement, the priests had a very significant role in Jewish society. By the time of Jesus, their teaching roles were being eclipsed somewhat by that of the scribes (whom we shall discuss below), but they still ideally commanded the respect of their countrymen. The Book of Malachi, written perhaps near the end of the fifth century BC, lays out the role of the ideal priest: "For the lips of a priest should preserve knowledge, and people should seek instruction from his mouth, because he is the messenger of the Lord of Hosts" (Mal 2:7). But by the time of Jesus, if they had not actually fallen from that pedestal, they were slouching severely.

The priesthood was a hereditary order. According to Exodus 28:1–2, Moses' brother Aaron was the father of the entire priesthood. All male descendants of Aaron (who were without some disqualifying physical defect; Lev 21:16–23) were able to serve as priests. (Aaron's tribe, the Levites, was responsible for assisting the priests in maintaining the Temple and sacrifices.) By the time of Jesus, there were many more priests than were actually necessary for the conduct of temple worship. Therefore, the priests were divided into twenty-four "courses," based on their family groups. According to rabbinic tradition, each course would serve for a week, the priests taking turns performing the needed sacrifices. The schedule repeated approximately twice a year. Certain duties, like the offering of the morning *tamid* sacrifice, were considered particularly honorable, and the priest who performed this task was chosen by lot from his brethren (as was Zechariah; Luke 1:8–9). The priests received a ration from the offerings while they served in Jerusalem. They also supported themselves through whatever professional pursuits they might choose.

Preeminence among the priests belonged to the high priest. The high priesthood was supposed to be a hereditary position, passed on from Aaron to his firstborn son, and through the firstborn sons throughout the generations. Ideally, there would never have been any question about who would serve as high priest. There were, however, many situations that could arise that could throw the matter into confusion, as when the high priest Eli's sons were killed in battle, followed immediately by Eli's own death (1 Samuel 4). Presumably, the nearest living relative would then take the post, although it is apparent from the biblical narrative that there were times when more than one candidate was available for the position. During the reign of David, Abiathar and Zadok both are prominent priests, though Abiathar seems to have functioned as the "high priest." As David lay on his deathbed, however, Abiathar supported David's son Adonijah for the throne, while Zadok supported Solomon. When Solomon succeeded his father to the throne, Zadok and his line were promoted to the high priesthood (1 Kgs 2:35). Zadok's line continued to supply this office until the time of the Hasmoneans, who usurped the position for themselves.

When Herod the Great had nearly eliminated the last of the Hasmoneans, he attempted to gut the significance of the high priesthood by appointing obscure figures to the office. As long as they met the minimal qualifications of being descended from Aaron, the legitimacy of these appointments could hardly be questioned, given the uncertainty of the succession at the time. This policy ended with Herod's death, and the priesthood regained its former prominence. In the time of Jesus, the high priests were appointed by the government authorities (governors or client kings, like Agrippa I) from a limited number of distinguished priestly families. The situation invited abuse, and bribes and political favors became an important part of the selection process.

THE SYNAGOGUE AND JEWISH PIETY

The Temple and priesthood may have constituted the focal point of the Jewish faith, but they had little impact on the daily religious life of the average Jew. For those living outside Judea, the Temple was a distant dream, a faraway place they longed to visit, but might never see. By the time of Jesus, Judaism had spread throughout the Mediterranean world, from Iran in the east to Spain in the west. There were major Jewish enclaves in Africa and Europe. Given the difficulties of long-distance travel in those days, no one could have expected the far-flung children of Abraham to conduct their worship in Jerusalem alone. Instead, synagogues became the centers of religious life, not only for the Diaspora Jews, but also for those living in Palestine. Each Sabbath day in communities throughout the Roman Empire, the Jewish people would come together for times of prayer, study, and celebration in buildings designated for this very purpose.

The origins of the synagogue are shrouded in mystery. The idea of community centers for prayer and study was unprecedented in the ancient world. Pagan shrines for various gods might be considered something of a distant cousin to the synagogue, but these sites were usually centers of sacrifice, not study. Many scholars argue that synagogues originated during the Babylonian Exile, as Jewish captives gathered together to study the words of the Law and the prophets, and to reinforce one another in their faith. With Solomon's Temple a ruin and Jerusalem a fading memory, the exiles would have needed the support of their community to encourage them to maintain their distinctive traditions, or they would have been assimilated among the Babylonians. The fact that the Jewish community survived and thrived is, in the view of many, persuasive evidence for the existence of some form of synagogue in those days.

But compelling as this scenario may be, there is no evidence supporting it. There is nothing in the Old Testament to indicate that the Jews of post-exilic times were in the habit of meeting together for formal study and worship in places designated for that purpose. Indeed, long after the Exile had ended, when Ezra wanted to expound the Mosaic laws to the Jewish population of Jerusalem, he did not go to a synagogue. Rather, a special assembly was called in the city square, where Ezra addressed the people (Ezra 8:2). It is certainly *possible* that Jews were meeting together in their own homes for prayer and study during the Babylonian Exile, but we can neither prove nor disprove that it was happening. The earliest real evidence for the existence of synagogues comes from the Greek period. In Egypt of the second century BC, we find references to the Jewish "houses of prayer"—the term commonly used for synagogues outside of Palestine in this era. By the first century AD, the practice had spread, and there is abundant evidence for the existence of local Jewish houses of worship in Palestine as well. In Palestinian Jewish sources, the building where the worshippers met was usually called a *synagoge* (Greek for "assembly"), and that title became the one most widely recognized.

The synagogue of those days bore little similarity to the church (or even the synagogue) of today. There was no minister in charge of proceedings. Rabbis—literally "great ones"—were not ministers in synagogues in the time of Jesus. In Jesus' day, the title "rabbi" was merely an honorary designation for a respected teacher. While rabbis could teach in synagogues, as both Jesus and Paul did, they possessed no official authority there. Rather, every adult male member of the synagogue community could take a turn reading the Scriptures and commenting on them if he chose to do so. Among the men attending synagogue, there was democracy.

Women and Gentiles were generally prohibited from reading or praying in the synagogue service. Many synagogues, however, allowed both women and Gentiles to attend services. Gentiles were segregated from the congregation, seated in a special section or balcony of the building. There has been much debate about whether Jewish women were segregated from the men, as in medieval synagogues, or if men and women were seated together. The evidence is inconclusive. There is some evidence, however, that even though women did not teach, they could fill some of the various leadership roles in the synagogues.

According to later rabbinic tradition, a synagogue could be established in any community where there was a quorum of ten Jewish men. A group of elders was in charge of maintaining order in the community, and could discipline the unruly with temporary expulsion or permanent excommunication from the assembly. In addition, each synagogue had an official called the *archisynagogos*, or "president of the assembly." This person, who may have been chosen from the elders, was primarily responsible for the order of worship. He would schedule readers, preachers, and prayer leaders. He also probably served as a trustee, maintaining the synagogue facilities. In addition, there could be minor officers in the synagogue, such as the person responsible for collections of charity. Such roles as these may have been filled by women.

The contents of the synagogue service seem to have been largely fixed already in Jesus' day. It began with the communal recitation of the Shema`: "Hear, O Israel, the Lord is our God; the Lord is one. And you shall love the Lord your God with all your heart, with all your soul, and with all your might" (Deut 6:4), along with other Scripture passages. This recitation was followed by a prayer, a reading from the Torah, a reading from the Prophets, and often a sermon. The readings could be accompanied by translations into Aramaic or Greek, depending on the needs of the congregation. Finally, if a priest or Levite was present, they would offer a closing blessing. Otherwise, the service ended with the reading of the Prophets.

THE SCRIBES

Apparently, the people often responsible for preaching in the synagogues would have been those known as "scribes." With the priesthood increasingly functioning as a political and ceremonial office, this group came to fill the role of popular teachers and community leaders. As a group, scribes had no official standing in Judaism. Their role seems to have evolved quite gradually, over a very long period of time. In Old Testament times, a "scribe" (Hebrew *sopher*) was a secretary, someone who was responsible for copying documents. In an era when literacy was rare, people skilled in reading and writing were very much in demand. They were recruited from various social strata, and some were actually slaves, specially trained for their literary responsibilities. Many were employed by temples or government, but private individuals could also employ scribes to draw up contracts. Nonetheless, since the literary skills often went hand in hand with other competencies, scribes' responsibilities often extended beyond just record keeping. Frequently, they functioned as officers of the king or governor. Ancient records often mention scribes who were not only given the responsibility of writing out orders, but of making sure that they were carried out, as well.

The Jewish idea of the scribe as a teacher seems to have derived from their role as copyists and compilers of the Mosaic laws. Undoubtedly their knowledge of the biblical texts led to the scribes becoming consultants in legal matters. This evolving role is well attested in Jewish literature of the Second Temple period. Ezra is described as a "scribe skilled in the law of Moses" (Ezra 7:6) and is given authority by the king of Persia to teach the laws to the people of Judah (7:25). The wise man Ben Sira (around 200 BC) describes the ideal scribe as a member of the leisure class, one who can "devote himself to reflecting on the laws of Moses" (Sir 39:1), who "reveals his learning in his teaching" (Sir 39:8) and thus will receive praise for his insight (Sir 39:9–11).[1] In 2 Baruch, written soon after AD 70, Jeremiah's scribe and companion Baruch is depicted as a leader of the Jewish community after the destruction of Jerusalem. The people look to him as a "father" (2 Bar 32:9) and depend upon him for instruction in the Mosaic law (46:2–3). It is apparent that by the time of the writing of 2 Baruch, the title "scribe" means far more than a mere transcriber or copyist.

In the New Testament, the word "scribes" is used for a group of people who opposed the teachings of Jesus. There is no historical evidence, however, that the "scribes" constituted any kind of formal association in this era. Rather, it seems that the term is used here for a class of people, a self-proclaimed "intelligentsia" or "academic elite." These people probably resented Jesus' popularity and the fact that he did not use the methods of biblical exposition that were widely recognized and respected. Instead of speaking in the name of earlier teachers and summarizing the old arguments, he taught as "one who has authority" (Matt 7:29).

THE PHARISEES

In the Gospel narratives, the scribes are usually found in close company with the Pharisees. Like the scribes, the Pharisees were devoted to the study of the Mosaic laws, and many of their number were recognized as teachers and community leaders. But unlike the scribes, the Pharisees constituted a cohesive faction with well defined beliefs. The basic outlines of these beliefs can be found in both the New Testament and the writings of Josephus, which seem to agree for the most part. Later rabbinic literature regards the Pharisees as the ancestors of the rabbis, and so we can cautiously project some of the rabbinic ideas back onto the Pharisees. But even with this supplemental material, there are still many questions about the origins, organization, and practices of this prominent Jewish sect.

---

1. We may contrast this description with Ben Sira's praise of the high priest Simon in Sir 50:1–21, which focuses exclusively on his ritual role, with no mention of teaching at all.

In Josephus's narrative, the Pharisees first make their appearance early in the Hasmonean era. In his *Antiquities of the Jews* 13:171–173, Josephus writes that there were three sects of Jews in those days, the Pharisees, the Sadducees, and the Essenes. The statement is probably an oversimplification, based on an analogy to the three most prominent schools of Greek philosophy (Stoicism, Epicureanism, and Skepticism). No doubt other groups existed as well, and many Jews did not identify with any particular religious sect. Mathematics alone makes the point obvious: Josephus claims that there were about 6,000 Pharisees in his day, and 4,000 Essenes, while the Sadducees comprised a small group of aristocrats. Since the Jewish population numbered in the millions in Jesus' day, these three sects together account for only a small fraction of the Jews living in those times. So we do not need to identify every Jew of the time as a Pharisee, Sadducee, or Essene, or to align every religious movement of the day with one of these sects; other factions were present and active throughout the era. They simply were not as important, or at least not as interesting to Josephus, as these three were.

Though the Pharisees comprised the largest and most influential of the sects, their origins are obscure. The sect's name apparently derives from the Hebrew verb *parash*, meaning "to separate." In the rabbinic texts, they are called the *perushim*—a passive form meaning "the separated ones." This name implies that the Pharisees had been separated from the other Jews. In that case, it seems somewhat ironic that Josephus considered the Pharisees to be the "people's party" in Jewish society. On the other hand, some scholars argue that the group took the name "Pharisee" because they were careful about making "separations" (distinctions) between people and things that were clean and unclean. Unlike those Jews who were lax about purity laws, the Pharisees insisted that every jot and tittle of the Law be scrupulously observed.

One of the most important characteristics of the Pharisees was their observance of what is often called "oral law." Both the Gospels and Josephus agree that the Pharisees adhered to a great body of teachings passed on through the ages (*Ant.* 13: 297; Mark 7:2–4). These *halakhot* (rules of conduct; singular *halakhah*) were traditional interpretations of the Laws of Moses. Somehow, they were considered binding on daily conduct, but they apparently lacked any official status. The body of oral law developed gradually, as Jewish sages debated the ambiguities of the biblical statutes. What constituted the "work" that Jews were commanded to refrain from on the Sabbath day? How should people "honor" their father and mother? How were Jewish festivals to be observed, especially outside the land of Judah? The Pharisaic teachers pondered such matters in depth, so they could provide clear guidelines for the Jewish people.

Aside from this preoccupation with *halakhah*, the Pharisees were also distinguished by what we might call their "theological" beliefs. In the passage from the *Antiquities* cited above, Josephus writes that the Pharisees believe some things in this world are caused by Fate, while others are left to human will. In other words, God willed some things to happen, but allowed for a certain amount of freedom.[2] Individuals are free to choose good or evil. And on the basis of that choice, the Pharisees argued, God would determine every person's eternal destiny. Those who had done good deeds would have eternal life, while the evil would suffer torment in hell (*Ant.* 18:14).

Josephus and the New Testament are somewhat conflicted on what the Pharisees believed happened after death. The New Testament states simply that the Pharisees believed in the resurrection of the dead (Acts 23:8). Josephus is a little more convoluted. In one passage, he states that the Pharisees believed the soul to be immortal, and that both good and evil souls descended to the underworld after death, where they received their rewards or punishments (*Ant.* 18:14). This description may well have been fashioned for the consumption of Josephus's Greek readers, who found the notion of the resurrection intolerable (see Acts 17:29–32). Earlier, Josephus had written that the Pharisees believed that righteous souls received a new body after their death (*War* 2:162). This position seems more compatible both with the Gospel accounts and with general Jewish beliefs of the age.

The New Testament tells us of another important Pharisaic belief: the Pharisees believed in angels and spirits, while the Sadducees did not (Acts 23:8). The precise meaning of this statement is hard to assess. Surely, we are not supposed to believe that Sadducees thought there were no such things as angels—their Bible would have included many stories of angelic visitations. Perhaps the matter here is that the Sadducees did not believe in angelic intervention in daily human affairs, or that the time of angels had passed. In any event, belief in angels proved to be a strong point of connection between the Christians and the Pharisees. The Pharisees in the Sanhedrin actually defended Paul against his ac-

---

2. The later rabbis held a similar view, according to the Mishnah (*m. Abot.* 3:16).

cusers by arguing that an angel or spirit might have spoken to him—a possibility the Sadducees apparently rejected (Acts 23:9).

Given the similarities between many Pharisaic beliefs and the teachings of Jesus and the early church, it might seem puzzling that the New Testament seems to hold the Pharisees in contempt (see, e.g., Matthew 23). There were several causes for the friction. First, the main point of contention between Jesus and the Pharisees involved the significance of the oral law. Jesus' approach to the ambiguities of Old Testament, according to the Gospels, was to emphasize the spirit or intention of the laws over the letter of the laws. For example, Jesus taught that the Sabbath was meant to be a day of rest and refreshment (see Mark 2:23–28), and therefore relieving pain or hunger on the Sabbath was perfectly acceptable. The Pharisees, on the other hand, emphasized that the Sabbath was a day for ceasing from work, and so the important issue was defining what constituted work, and rigidly following the rules. Jesus, to them, was a law breaker, and his teachings threatened the very existence of the Jewish nation. Jesus, for his part, considered many of the Pharisees to be hypocrites. They were inflexible about matters like tithing or keeping kosher, but were willing to wink on matters like forgiveness and compassion for the poor (Matt 23:23).

The early church, too, continued to butt heads with the Pharisees. In Palestine, the Pharisees had a certain appeal to the common people. According to Josephus, the masses generally accepted the Pharisees' teachings and leadership (*Ant.* 18:15–17). To those who asked, "What does God want of me?", they had a straightforward and explicit answer: obey these laws, and you shall live. Even though the rules may have seemed burdensome, they were at least clear. Christians, however, offered a different answer to these common folks. It was not through keeping the laws they would be saved, but by putting trust in Jesus as Messiah. As the gospel message began to draw many Jews away from scrupulous obedience to the Law, it was inevitable that the Christians and Pharisees would come into conflict. As Christianity began its mission among the Gentiles, it found itself in even greater conflict with the Pharisees. Apparently the Pharisees were actively involved in proselytizing converts in those days (see Matt 23:15), but they only enjoyed partial success. There were many converts to Judaism, but there were also many Gentiles who became "God-fearers," unwilling to undergo full conversion. Christianity seemed to offer a good compromise: you could have the morals and beliefs of Judaism without the legalistic baggage. There in the greater Mediterranean world, the two sects seemed to be heading for a showdown. The tide apparently turned against Pharisaism after the Jewish revolts of AD 66 and AD 130, which magnified general Roman antipathy against Judaism.

We do well to keep this context in mind as we read the Gospel narratives. Some scholars and popular writers have accused the Gospels of being anti-Semitic, and distorting the Judaism of Jesus' day. But these charges fail to take into account the fact that most of the New Testament authors were themselves Jewish. The Gospel writers did not direct their criticisms against Judaism in general, but against the leaders and the groups with whom they clashed most fiercely. Even when the Gospel of John, for example, speaks disparagingly of "the Jews," it usually means only the Jewish political establishment. On the other hand, popular teachers often paint all Pharisees with the same brush, as if they were the epitome of hypocrisy. Pharisaism, for all its faults, represented a sincere effort to understand God's will for the Jewish people. Occasionally, the Bible depicts Pharisees like Nicodemus, Joseph of Arimathea, and Gamaliel in a more favorable light.

THE SADDUCEES

The Sadducees play a much smaller part in New Testament narratives than the Pharisees do, but their direct impact on Jesus was greater. As leaders of the Temple establishment in Jesus' time (Acts 4:1-4, 5:17-18) and as the socio-economic elites of Palestinian Jewish society, it was the Sadducees who were most directly threatened by Jesus' message and popularity.

According to Josephus, the Sadducees constituted a small, aristocratic sect from the highest economic stratum of Judean society. And like aristocrats in many societies, they were social and religious conservatives. While the Pharisees were adaptive in their approach to the Jewish law, interpreting regulations as literally, figuratively, or loosely as the case might seem to demand, the Sadducees were rigid adherents to the plain sense of Scripture. Josephus writes that they rejected oral tradition, and observed nothing that could not be directly demonstrated from the Law of Moses (*Ant.* 13:297, 18:16). We must take this statement with a grain of salt: there can be no doubt that the Sadducees had traditions of their own that guided their interpretations of the Law. But apparently Josephus believed that the Sadducees did not assign the same authority to their oral traditions that the Pharisees did. They preferred to stick close to the plain meaning of the text.

Some scholars have argued that Josephus's statement might have more far-reaching significance. Does their insistence on sticking to "the law of Moses" imply that the Sadducees accepted only the five Books of Moses—Genesis, Exodus, Leviticus, Numbers, and Deuteronomy—as Scripture? Such a position would not be without precedent. The Samaritans' Bible included only the Books of Moses, as well. Furthermore, if the Sadducees only recognized the authority of the Pentateuch, it would explain why Jesus, when debating with the Sadducees over the issue of the resurrection of the dead, did not refer them to the explicit statements about the resurrection in Daniel 12 or the resurrection imagery in Ezekiel 37 or Psalms 16 and 49. Instead, he refuted them with Exodus 3:6, a passage from the Books of Moses: "I am the God of Abraham, the God of Isaac, and the God of Jacob" (Matt 22:23–32).

According to the New Testament and Josephus, the Sadducees rejected the idea of resurrection of the dead. In fact, Josephus does not even attribute to them a belief in a spiritual afterlife. Apparently, according to the Sadducees, death was the final word on human existence (which, according to the old joke, is why they were "Sad, you see"). Their lack of faith in the afterlife might partially explain their apparent devotion to worldly comfort. Without hope of a "world to come," the Sadducees believed that divine rewards and punishments would come in this world. If they were wealthy, it meant God was pleased with them. If they were poor, it meant they must be doing something wrong. The Sadducees had no qualms about enjoying the benefits of wealth and power in life, because these gifts were the wages of righteous living. None of our sources ever accuse the Sadducees as a group of impiety or immorality, only of arrogance and ignorance.

Another detail that Josephus relates is that the Sadducees rejected the notion of "Fate" (*Ant.* 13:171–173). In other words, they did not believe that God directed human affairs. No doubt Josephus exaggerates their position somewhat. No one who believed the books of Moses could doubt that God intervenes in human affairs. Nor would there be any reward for righteousness if God did not recompense human deeds. It seems more likely that the Sadducees rejected any notion of predestination: God does not direct or foreknow human decisions, so human beings would be wholly responsible for their actions. It is also possible that the Sadducees believed that the days of divine intervention had passed. We have already noted that the New Testament tells us that the Sadducees did not believe in angels or spirits (Acts 23:9). Again, if the Sadducees believed the stories of the Pentateuch, they would have known that angels had visited the earth. Perhaps they simply believed that the days of angels, spirits, and miraculous manifestations were passed.

The Sadducees seem to have had an especially close relationship with the Temple and its personnel. In fact, the very name "Sadducee" might imply a connection with the traditional high priesthood. "Saddouk" is the Greek form of the Hebrew name "Zadok," meaning "righteous." The name "Zadok" was fairly common in intertestamental times, so "Zadok" could simply have been the name of the group's forgotten founder. But on the other hand, the name Zadok had special significance in the early Hasmonean era when the Sadducean sect came into existence. Since the days of King Solomon, the high priests had traditionally been drawn from the Zadok family. When the Hasmoneans came into power, they ousted the traditional "Zadokite" (or, as spelled in Greek, "Sadducee") line. The sect of the Sadducees might have been partisans of the displaced Zadokite high priests.

But a caveat is in order: the connection between the high priesthood and the Sadducees is not always clear. Josephus only explicitly identifies only one high priest, Ananus, as a Sadducee (*Ant.* 20:199), and he seems to imply that some of them were actually allied with the Pharisees (see, e.g., *Ant.* 17:149–167). It is apparent that not all priests, and not even all high priests, were Sadducees. But in the time of Jesus, the high priestly "establishment" is explicitly identified with the Saducean party (Acts 4:1-4, 5:17-18). These people had directly profited from the "money-changing" that Jesus had attacked. They also had much to lose if Jesus actually initiated a rebellion against Rome, as many Jews believed the Messiah would do. There is no reason to doubt that the Sadducees were deeply complicit in the execution of Christ.

One final point should be noted on relations between the Pharisees and Sadducees. In rabbinic literature, there are several references to conflicts between the two groups. Given their very different views on resurrection and free will, we might not be surprised. What *is* surprising, however, is that the recorded conflicts usually have little to do with theology *per se*. Rather, the major disagreements between Pharisees and Sadducees are characterized as matters of interpreting ritual law, or *halakhah*. We do have to view this picture with some skepticism, because in the rabbinic literature, Sadducees are treated as little more than "straw men" to be dispatched by clever Pharisees. But if there is any historicity to the disputes, then the Pharisees probably would have been more forgiving of the Sadducees' rejecting the doctrine of resurrection than, say, their methods of washing their hands before meals. Judaism has always tended to put more emphasis on proper actions ("orthopraxis") than proper beliefs ("orthodoxy"), whereas Christianity has tended to switch those emphases around. The stress on correct theology would come to distinguish Christianity from the other Jewish groups of the first century.

ESSENES

The Pharisees and Sadducees are the only Jewish sects mentioned in the New Testament, but as noted above, they were not the only ones in existence in Jesus' day. Josephus and Philo of Alexandria both devote a good deal of space to descriptions of the Essenes and their practices (Josephus: *Ant.* 18:18–22; *War* 2:119–161; Philo: *Every Good Man Is Free* 12:75–87; *Hypothetica* 11:1–8). The Essenes were not the largest or most influential of the sects; rather, the attention they get derives from the fact that they were the *strangest* of the sects. Living in communes, dressing in white, abstaining from marriage, refusing to hold slaves, the Essenes were something of an oddity among the Jews (although similar communal groups did exist elsewhere in the ancient world). According to Josephus, they rejected the notion of free will, believing all things to be predestined by God—conveniently filling out the spectrum from total free will (Sadducees) to some free will (Pharisees) to no free will (Essenes). Josephus also attributes to them a Platonic belief in the immortality of the soul—that the soul existed before birth, and was released at death to return to heaven. Once again, their theology seems to mediate between that of the Sadducees (no afterlife) and Pharisees (bodily resurrection). One might suspect that Josephus has "massaged his data" a bit, since the system seems to work out a little *too* neatly.

The Essenes never appear in the New Testament. Theories of an earlier day that identified Jesus and John the Baptist as Essenes are largely discounted these days. Essene roles in Jewish history after the time of Jesus are minor. They never appear in rabbinic literature, having disappeared well before the third century AD. Many scholars would identify the Dead Sea Scrolls Community as "Essene." There are, indeed, several similarities between the group described in some of the Scrolls and the Essenes of Josephus and Philo (as well as some significant differences). But caution is due here: there were undoubtedly many different Jewish groups in existence in this period besides Pharisees, Sadducees, and Essenes, and it is probably unnecessary and perhaps a little presumptuous to identify the Scrolls sect with this group when neither the word "Essene," nor any possible Hebrew or Aramaic equivalents, ever appear in the Scrolls.

If we leave aside the possible identification of the Essenes with the Dead Sea Scrolls Community, the Essenes are little more than a historical curiosity, one of those radical splinter groups that capture human imagination, but do little of lasting significance. Since they had no apparent impact on the life and ministry of Jesus, we will not let them detain us any longer.

THE FOURTH PHILOSOPHY

In contrast, a sect that *does* have a serious impact on New Testament and Jewish history is one that Josephus identifies as "the Fourth Philosophy" (Pharisees, Sadducees, and Essenes being the other three). According to Josephus, this group began around AD 6 or 7, when the Roman governor Quirinius instituted a new tax on the Jews. Founded by "Judas the Galilean" and a Pharisee named Saddouk, the group adopted many of the Pharisees' beliefs. This sect, however, had an unquenchable desire for freedom, and refused to acknowledge any kingship but God's (*Ant.* 18:23). They promoted riots and general civil unrest throughout most of the first century AD, culminating in the Great Revolt and the destruction of the Temple in AD 70. Very likely, they were motivated by religious factors as much as political grievances. They believed, like Jesus, that the Kingdom of God was about to make its appearance on earth. Unlike Jesus, however, they believed that the conquest of the kingdoms of this world would require militant participation of the Jewish people.

In the Gospel accounts of Jesus' ministry, this resistance movement is the elephant in the living room whose presence is often felt, but not explicitly acknowledged.[3] Jesus' teachings on non-retaliation (e.g., Matt.

---

3. It is often mistakenly stated that one of Jesus' disciples, "Simon the Zealot," was

5:38–47) were directed against those who were fomenting hatred and active resistance. Jesus' teachings on the Kingdom of God promoted a vision of revolution that was spiritual and apolitical. His understanding of his messianic mission contrasted sharply with that promoted by the Fourth Philosophy.

MESSIANISM

This point brings us to our discussion of Jewish messianic expectations. Often oversimplified, misunderstood, or misrepresented, messianism was as diverse as any other aspect of Jewish religion in Jesus' day. We cannot simply say that Jesus was rejected because "the Jews were seeking a militant messiah, and Jesus was a man of peace." While some of the Jewish people were indeed seeking a warlord-savior, many other ideas were circulating at the time.

The roots of Jewish messianism stretch deep into biblical antiquity. Even the word "messiah" is ancient, being an English rendering of the Hebrew word *mashiach*, meaning "anointed one." In Old Testament times, people who were installed into special offices, such as kings, priests, and prophets, were symbolically anointed with special oil as a sign of their new position and new relationship with God (e.g., Lev 8:10–12; 1 Sam 10:1). Later, the term "anointed one" came to mean anyone divinely ordained for a special office, whether they had literally been smeared with oil or not (see Psa 105:15). But the term "the Messiah," as a title for a supernatural deliverer, does not appear in any Old Testament texts. It is not until New Testament times that the title "the Messiah" comes into prominence in Judaism. The title of Jesus, "Christ," is simply a Greek translation of the same word: *christos*, "anointed one."

The concept of the Messiah as a God-ordained king and deliverer of the Jewish nation has both biblical and historical roots. Its biblical origins ultimately lie in the covenant that God established with King David. According to 2 Samuel 7, David had desired to build a permanent temple to house the Ark of the Covenant, but God answered through the prophet Nathan that it would be David's son, not David, who would undertake that project. But because of David's piety, God promised that

---

a member of the Jewish freedom movement. While there was in fact a group of rebels known as the Zealots, that group was founded by a figure named John of Gischala in AD 66—long after the time of Jesus. Simon was probably just zealous for his Jewish faith, not for violence.

he would establish David's dynasty perpetually (2 Sam 7:16). The moral failings of David's descendants, however, seemed to cast that prospect in doubt. If God did not spare the northern kingdom Israel because of its kings' wickedness, how could Judah escape the same fate? Already in the eighth century BC, prophets were anticipating the coming of a special Davidic king who would lead the nation in true obedience to the Lord (e.g., Mic 5:1-5; Isa 9:1-7, 11:1-10). These hopes intensified in the waning days of Judah's monarchy and burned brightly during the Babylonian Exile (see Jer 23:5-6, 30:39; Ezek 34:23-24, 37:24-25). But as decades of foreign rule stretched into centuries, hope for the coming of this Davidic "super-king" seemed to dwindle.

Political events, however, resurrected those latent hopes. When the Hasmonean Revolt brought about a new Jewish dynasty, Israel's national pride was re-ignited. But this new monarchy was not without a dark side: not only were the Hasmoneans not of David's line, they also demonstrated a marked tendency toward ruthlessness and immorality. When the Hasmonean regime fell to the Romans in 63 BC, many in Judea breathed a sigh of relief—but the taste for independence remained upon their tongues. The covenant that God had made with King David and the promises of the prophets experienced a renaissance. One of the so-called Psalms of Solomon, written in this era, condemns the Hasmoneans as usurpers who only got what they deserved. But then it adds: "Look, O Lord, and raise up for them their king, the son of David, at the time known to you, O God, so that he may reign over Israel your servant. Gird him with strength, so he may shatter unrighteous rulers, and purge Jerusalem from gentiles trampling her to destruction."[4] The Dead Sea Scrolls, too, often allude to the Old Testament messianic prophecies. In the Dead Sea Scroll Community's interpretations, the coming Davidic monarch was called "the Prince of the congregation." His primary task, apparently, was to lead the righteous Jews into victory over the Gentiles and their wicked Jewish allies.

These documents seem to anticipate the coming of a human messiah, apparently attributing to him no supernatural powers except his invincibility. And this was probably the messianic concept shared by most Jews who were expecting the advent of David's illustrious descendant. But there were other ideas circulating, as well—ideas inspired by different biblical texts, and nurtured in various Jewish circles. Zechariah's

---

4. PsaSol. 17:21-22. Translation by Wright, "Psalms of Solomon," 666.

prophecies about the glorification of the high priest (e.g., Zech 3:1–7, 6:9–15), along with the dynasty of the priest-king Hasmoneans, encouraged in some quarters the notion of a priestly messiah who would purge the sins of Israel and restore perfect righteousness. According to some of the Dead Sea Scrolls, the priestly messiah would serve as co-ruler with the Davidic messiah. Other texts (e.g., the Aramaic "Testament of Levi," also found among the Dead Sea Scrolls) speak only of a priestly ruler.

But the Book of Daniel provided some of the most fertile imagery for messianic speculation. Daniel 12:1 tells how in a time of crisis, the archangel Michael would arise to deliver Israel. Some interpreters understood this verse to mean that the Jewish people should look not to humanity but to heaven for the deliverance of Judah. Perhaps a divine being would descend and deliver them in their time of greatest need. Josephus tells us that during the siege of Jerusalem, some of the city residents took refuge on the roof of the Temple to watch for "signs of their deliverance" (*War* 6:283–286). On the other hand, some interpreters seemed to expect an incarnation of an angel. The Melchizedek scroll from Qumran Cave 11 seems to envision an incarnate Michael leading the righteous into their final victory over the nations. The first chapter of the Book of Hebrews may well have been written to address this belief.

But more influential still was the "Son of Man" passage in Daniel 7. In this chapter, the prophet Daniel sees a vision of four beasts representing a succession of world empires. But in the time of the final kingdom, Daniel sees "one like a Son of Man" coming with the clouds of heaven. This figure is presented before God, and given dominion over all the earth and eternal kingship. The interpretation that Daniel received was, in one sense, plain enough: the vision foretold the coming of the Kingdom of God to ultimately do away with the kingdoms of the earth. But on the other hand, it left a great deal of "wiggle room" for its interpreters. Who was the "Son of Man?" Was he an individual—an angel (perhaps Michael), or the Messiah? Or was he simply a symbol of the reign of God, just as the beasts were symbols of earthly kingdoms? At various times, interpreters (both ancient and modern) have argued for each of these understandings of the vision. But some influential Jewish texts from around the time of Jesus (1 Enoch, 4 Ezra) explicitly identified this Son of Man as the Messiah. What is more, they deduced from Daniel's vision that this Messiah must be more than a mere human. He appeared with the clouds, indicating his heavenly origins. He was given dominion, apparently without having to fight for it, suggesting a supernatural power to vanquish his enemies. He was presented before God and given a throne, making him in some sense (in some interpretations, at least) comparable to God himself.

These various interpretations of the messianic expectation had some important practical implications. Those who were expecting a Davidic warlord, an invincible human messiah, might well be persuaded to take up arms in the cause of a revolutionary leader who demonstrated some early success. Several such figures appeared in the time of Jesus, and they brought a great deal of mischief in their wake (see Acts 5:35-39). Those who expected a heavenly deliverer, on the other hand, would be more inclined to wait patiently for their salvation. God would bring the Messiah in his own time, and human efforts would accomplish little. Those whose messianic expectations combined various ideas—perhaps a human messiah with some kind of divine origin—might be motivated to follow a miracle worker, someone who possessed superhuman powers. The Jewish people seemed to be in almost constant unrest during the first couple centuries of Roman rule, and messianic expectations undoubtedly played a big part in the agitation.

CONCLUSION

Jewish religion in Jesus' time was a variegated collage of ideas, practices, and opinions. There was only the barest core of "normative Judaism," an orthodox set of beliefs that defined who was truly Jewish and who was not. But there was no central authority—not even the high priesthood—that had the power to impose its beliefs on the Jewish people. And so, the different factions competed for the hearts of the people by promising the favor of God and hope for the future. Sometimes, the conflicts between the factions turned violent. During the Hasmonean era, both the Pharisees and Sadducees took their turn at persecuting their rival sect. The Dead Sea Scrolls community relates in the Damascus Document how its founder, the Teacher of Righteousness, was driven into exile by someone called the "wicked priest." But more often, it seems, the various strands of Judaism managed to coexist, recognizing that the things that bound them together were more substantial than those that tore them apart. Belief in the Lord, obedience to his Law, and commitment to his Temple in Jerusalem were the true touchstones of Jewish identity in the time of Jesus.

8

Jesus in His "Place"

According to the doctrine of the Trinity, Jesus was fully human and fully divine. He was not God in human disguise; he was not half God and half man. He was as much a part of our world as he was of Heaven. He lived as people live, in time and space. So while the study of Jesus' divinity belongs to the realm of the theologian, his humanity can be investigated by historians in the same way that we can study Alexander the Great or Julius Caesar.

In this chapter, we will revisit the biblical story of Jesus' life and work, making some explicit references to the historical and cultural background that has been the subject of this study. We will pay special attention to some issues that have been the subject of controversy among scholars, or a possible source of confusion for faithful Bible readers.

BIRTH AND CHILDHOOD

Jesus was born in Palestine during the reign of the Roman Emperor Augustus. In our current calendar, Jesus' birth is said to have occurred in 1 AD, the first "year of Our Lord" (there is no "Year Zero"). But it now seems likely that the calendars are wrong. The traditional date derives from the calculations of a monk named Dionysius Exiguus who lived in the sixth century AD. The monk's system proved to be popular and gained wide acceptance in Christendom, but its accuracy has recently come into question. As discussed in Chapter 4, scholars now generally agree that Herod the Great died shortly before Passover in 4 BC. Since the Gospel accounts of Matthew and Luke agree that Herod was ruling Judea when Jesus was born, the Nativity must have actually occurred several years "before Christ." Typically, the figure now used for the year of Jesus' birth is 6 BC, in the last phases of Herod's reign.

Luke tells us that Jesus was born in Bethlehem because Joseph had to travel there for a census taken when Quirinius was governor of Syria (Luke 2:2-5). There has been much disagreement about whether or not this explanation should be considered historical. First, there is the problem of whether Caesar could have ordered a census in the realm of an "allied king" like Herod. While Augustus was known to use censuses to be sure that the tax burden was fairly distributed among his realms, typically, he would not have interfered in the internal affairs of a kingdom with "allied" status. The other problem concerns the mention of Quirinius: according to Josephus, Quirinius did not become governor of Syria until AD 6-7. At that time, he initiated a census of Judea that set off riots among the Jews. Many scholars believe that Luke has misdated the census of Quirinius by twelve years, mistakenly seizing upon it as an explanation for the Holy Family's pilgrimage to Bethlehem.

Several possible solutions to the problem have been proposed, short of rejecting Luke's account altogether. First, it is not impossible that Herod could have agreed to (or even requested) a census for the good of his realm. Given his great willingness to please his overlords, Herod would hardly have objected to Augustus's efforts to see that tax burdens were equitably distributed throughout his realm. And as for Quirinius, it has been suggested that he may have governed Syria twice, or that he may have held a different administrative office in the East before becoming governor of Syria. It has even been suggested that the solution to the problem may be grammatical, rather than historical: the Greek preposition used in Luke's account can be understood to mean that the census occurred *before* Quirinius was governor. We may not be able to make a definitive judgment, but there are plenty of possible solutions to the problem of Quirinius's census.

Matthew records the story of the star of Bethlehem that guided the Magi to the baby Jesus. While the Old Testament was quite disdainful of those who observed the stars and other celestial phenomena, Jewish attitudes had changed significantly during the intertestamental times. We have noted how the Greeks tried to put astrology on a more "scientific" footing. The presence of horoscopes among the Dead Sea Scrolls demonstrates that astrology was finding acceptance in Jesus' day even among conservative Jewish groups. The idea of seeking guidance from a star, then, would have been readily accepted by the Jews of Jesus' day.

According to Matthew, it was the Magi's visit that alerted Herod to the presence of a new king in his realm and prompted the Slaughter of the Innocents. Scholars often dismiss the Slaughter as legend, since it is not recorded in Josephus or other ancient sources. But given the paranoia and ruthlessness that characterized the latter days of Herod's reign, the story is hardly out of character. Someone who would have murdered all the dignitaries of Judea just to ensure that there would be mourning at his death would surely not have spared some infants who might pose a threat to his kingdom. Furthermore, it should be noted that Bethlehem probably had fewer than a thousand residents in those days, in which case the incident would have involved only a couple dozen children at most. In such violent and turbulent times when the destruction of entire communities could occur with little notice from outsiders, the death of some infants could easily have escaped the interest of historians—especially in the Greco-Roman world, where infants were routinely killed simply because they presented an inconvenience to their parents.

It is not surprising that Jesus' childhood was mostly ignored by the Gospels. Childhood was, after all, largely considered insignificant in the ancient world. The only exception occurs in the Gospel of Luke. Luke includes an incident that occurred when Jesus was twelve years old, where he astounded the teachers in the Temple with his wisdom (Luke 2:41–51). In the context of Luke's Gospel, this detail is almost expected. Luke patterned his account of Jesus' life after Hellenistic biographies that were popular in those days. It was common practice among Greco-Roman biographers that when chronicling the lives of great men, they would include an incident from their childhood that foreshadowed their future greatness. Herodotus tells of how the child Cyrus had acted like a king over other children (*Histories* 1:114–116); Plutarch tells how young Alexander would amaze his elders with his eloquence (*Alexander* 5); and even Josephus recounts how he, as a boy, was consulted by the learned men on fine points of Jewish law (*Life* 2:9).

We can assume that Jesus was trained in the Scriptures by his father Joseph, since it was a father's duty to impart such knowledge to Jewish boys. But almost as important was the teaching of a trade, and we can assume that Jesus learned the skills of carpentry from Joseph, as well (Matt 13:55). The work of a carpenter required a good deal of vigor. It was heavy labor, allowing little time for leisure or contemplation. Nor was it likely to make anyone rich. Carpenters were not highly regarded in Greco-Roman society, and Jesus' background made him suspect to his audiences (Matt 13:53-57; Mark 6:2-4).

Some writers have claimed that Jesus had extensive contact with Gentiles during his boyhood in Galilee, and this contact led him to become more charitable to non-Jews than the Pharisees or other groups of the age would have been. There are some problems with this line of reasoning. First, while Jesus does demonstrate a benevolent attitude toward some of the Gentiles he encountered in his ministry, we should not idealize his position. Like others of his day, he sometimes makes a strong distinction between the Gentiles and the Jews. For example, he forbids his disciples from going to Gentile cities (Matt 12:5); he initially gives a strong rebuff to a Gentile woman seeking his aid (Matt 15:21-28); and he tells the Samaritan woman at the well that "salvation is of the Jews" (John 4:22). These attitudes were understandable given the focus of Jesus' ministry among the Jewish people, and we should not feel compelled to apologize for him, or to make him appear more liberal minded than he really was. Furthermore, the openness that Jesus does demonstrate toward Gentiles was not especially unusual among the Jews of this time. As we have noted, Gentiles were permitted entry into the outer courts of the Temple in Jerusalem, and were welcome in synagogues even if they refused to convert. We might also note that the later rabbis were generally charitable toward Gentiles, conceding that those who kept the covenant of Noah (abstaining from idolatry, blasphemy, murder, sexual immorality, and eating blood) would be accepted by God.

Finally, the notion that Jesus would have been exposed to many Gentiles as a boy growing up in Galilee is certainly open to challenge. The population of Galilee was predominantly Jewish, and the typical Jew would probably have avoided the Greek cities of the realm. Many scholars, however, believe that Jesus and his father were employed in the rebuilding of the important Palestinian city of Sepphoris in AD 19. In such a case, Jesus may have had opportunities to work beside people of various ethnic backgrounds. But even in this important city, the Gentile population does not seem to have constituted anything like a majority in the time of Jesus.

THE BEGINNING OF JESUS' MINISTRY

The Gospels tell us that Jesus' ministry dovetailed into that of John the Baptist, perhaps the most famous religious reformer of his day. Before beginning his ministry, Jesus was "baptized" by John as a sign of repentance. The significance of the baptism ritual is uncertain. It may have been an intensified version of Jewish ritual bathing, the *mikvah*. Jews would undergo ritual baths when they had come into contact with something unclean, so baptism may simply have been a sign that the people felt they were unclean because of their sins, and needed to be made pure. On the other hand, some have associated the practice with the rituals used for initiating Gentile converts into the Jewish faith. After they had undergone a period of training and probation, proselytes were immersed in a *mikvah* of running water in order to wash away the impurities of their former lifestyle. We cannot say for certain what baptism meant for John and his disciples, though it was certainly a sign of repentance. In any case, John felt that Jesus did not actually need to be baptized, since he had no need to repent.

After his baptism, Jesus went out into the "Judean Wilderness." It would have been an excellent place to fast, given that most of the year, there was almost nothing to eat here. Probably Jesus took shelter from the sun in the caves like those near Qumran. These same caves would provide refuge later for Jews fleeing from the Roman forces during the first revolt (AD 67–74) and the Bar Kochba rebellion (AD 130–135). Later still, St. Anthony (third century AD) would retreat to similar caves in search for a quiet place to pursue God, thus giving birth to the Christian monastic movement.

JESUS' MESSAGE

Jesus' ministry was primarily centered in Galilee, which was a hotbed of anti-Roman sentiment in the first century. This fact probably influenced much of Jesus' teaching. In Jesus' day, Jewish expectations of the advent of the Kingdom of God were running rampant. There were a couple factors fueling these expectations. The first was the success of the Hasmonean Dynasty, which had resurrected hopes for a free Jewish state. The taste of liberty had not yet departed from Jewish tongues in Jesus' time. The other factor was the apparent fulfillment of Bible passages like Daniel 7, which speaks of an evil world-dominating empire that suffers its downfall at the rise of the people of God. To many Jews, Daniel's description of the doomed empire sounded much like the kingdom currently ruling the world—the Roman Empire. Rome's success was only temporary, for the righteous Jews were destined to strike out and overthrow the Roman

Empire by the power of their God. Jesus, however, interpreted God's Kingdom in a different manner. For him, the Kingdom was not a political entity carved out with swords of steel. Instead, it would be a spiritual realm, won not with weapons but with the words of the gospel (John 18:36). Its ethics included a commitment to non-retaliation even against those who would harm or oppress the Jews (Matt 5:38–47).

According to John's Gospel, Jesus' travels took him through Samaria on his way to Judea. Although this route was the direct, logical way of getting between the lands, many Jews would rather have traveled far out of their way rather than pass through this hostile territory. Here, in the Samaritan village of Sychar, Jesus had his conversation with a Samaritan woman at a well (John 4). In their conversation, they both correctly identify the core issue of contention between the Jews and the Samaritans: Jews felt sacrificial worship should be conducted in Jerusalem, while Samaritans felt it should take place on Mt. Gerizim (4:20). Jesus' answer that the place was not as significant as the spirit of worship probably anticipated the destruction of the Jerusalem Temple in AD 70. In any event, it indicated that the issues separating Jews and Samaritans were not so irreconcilable as both parties seemed to believe.

Jesus often made reference to the customs of his day in his teaching. In the Gospels, Jesus' conflicts with the Pharisees generally center on issues like ritual purification and Sabbath observance. Jesus took a relaxed position on the ritual laws: such issues are secondary aspects of God's law, whose core, after all, is the love of God and neighbor. But the Pharisees had a different understanding of the significance of these ordinances. To them, they were the distinctives that made the Jews God's holy people. In the days of the Antiochan persecution, Jews had sacrificed their lives rather than eat pork or defile their Sabbath rest. It must have enraged them that Jesus could put so little stock in such matters. Likewise, Jesus' teachings on divorce (Matt 19:3–9) reflected a significant ideological conflict of his day. While the major rabbinic figures debated the conditions when divorce was permitted, Jesus argued that God never intended divorce at all—the allowance was a concession to sinful human nature. Jesus' strict guidelines would have placed him at odds not only with the famous Rabbi Hillel, but also with the typical practice of the day, as illustrated by Josephus and ancient manuscript discoveries.

Much of Jesus' message for his generation was embedded in parables. Jesus should not be credited with inventing this teaching method:

the Greek teacher Aesop (620–560 BC) used stories to illustrate truths long before the time of Jesus, and both Jewish and Gentile teachers continued to use the method into Jesus' day and beyond. Often, Jesus' stories refer to both historical events and cultural features that would have been especially cogent to his first-century Jewish audience. When Jesus speaks of a ruler who went on a trip to receive a kingdom for himself (Luke 19:12), he was no doubt referring to Archelaus, son of Herod the Great, who traveled to Rome expecting to be made ruler of his father's realm. When he said, "A city which is set on a hill cannot be hidden" (Matt 5:14), he might well have been referring to Sepphoris, a mere five miles from his home, located on a hill and visible from a great distance. One of his most famous parables, the Prodigal Son (Luke 15:11–32), alludes to the inheritance customs of his day, in which the father distributes his wealth to his children before his death. The parable of the wise and foolish virgins (Matt 25:1–13), while its basic message may be understood by anyone, can only be fully appreciated by those who have an understanding of Jewish wedding customs of the first century, where the groom would proceed through town to the home of his betrothed to claim her and take her back to the home he had prepared for her. Likewise, shepherds and their ways, while foreign to the experience of most modern Westerners, were well known in ancient times. Jesus' use of these figures as object lessons may have seemed a little "subversive," to some extent at least, since shepherds were generally considered an untrustworthy lot in those days.

THE MIRACLES

While the miracles of Jesus do not have the same kind of historical connections that we find in his teaching, they often can only fully be appreciated in light of his cultural environment. Take his exorcisms, for example. In our own day, exorcisms are pretty rare events. In Jesus' day, however, there was more openness to the idea of demonic possession as a cause for both physical and emotional disorders. The existence of demons was taken for granted, it seems, by nearly everyone, and they were feared. Exorcists were highly trained specialists in the expulsion of these malevolent beings, masters of a significant branch of the magical arts. Exorcism was not considered a job for amateurs (see Acts 19:11–17). The rituals were often long and involved, and frequently unsuccessful.

Jesus' approach to exorcism was significantly unique. He did not invoke magic chants, burn herbs, or wrestle with the possessed. Rather, it was his mere word that drove the demons from their hosts. This was not a mere quantitative difference—i.e., a more powerful magic. Rather, this was a demonstration of full authority over the powers of darkness. In the Gospels, Jesus' power to drive out evil spirits was nothing less than a sign that the kingdom of God was coming, and the kingdom of the Devil had already been defeated.

Jesus' healing miracles have a similar theological significance. Jesus associated them with his role as Messiah. When John the Baptist sent messengers asking Jesus if he was the Messiah, he replied, "Return and report to John what you have seen and heard: The blind have their sight restored, the lame walk, the lepers are cleansed, and the deaf hear, the dead are raised, and the good news is proclaimed to the poor. And blessed is the one who does not stumble on account of me" (Luke 7:22-23). Jesus was clearly alluding here to Isaiah 61:1, where the messenger proclaims that his works of mercy demonstrated the arrival of "the year of the Lord's favor." Such miracles—which were no doubt uncommon in Jesus' day—were a sign to John and to others that the "end of the age" had come, just as the prophets had predicted.

In the time of Jesus, sickness was often associated with sin. This fact lay behind Jesus' occasional admonitions to those he had healed that they needed to stop sinning (John 5:14; see also Mark 2:5). In these cases, Jesus was able to go beyond the actions of earlier prophets by not only offering healing, but forgiveness, as well (Mark 2:5). Furthermore, Jesus sometimes puzzled his disciples by contending that some sickness had nothing to do with sin (John 9:1-3). He did not associate all diseases with spiritual infirmities or powers, and acknowledged that physicians have their place for treating disease (Matt 9:12). His ideas regarding sickness both reflected and rejected some of the common conceptions of his day.

The same may be said of Jesus' treatment of some of the diseases that carried social stigmas in his society. The woman with a hemorrhage of blood (Matt 9:18-22) would have been perpetually excluded from the Jewish community, since any blood flow was considered to be defiling. Jesus treated the woman with compassion after she had been healed by touching his garment. Also, no disease was considered more defiling than the skin diseases commonly (and inaccurately) called "leprosy."

Often regarded as a sure sign of divine disfavor (see Num 12:1–15; 2 Kgs 15:5; 2 Chron 26:16–20), lepers were segregated from Jewish society and excluded from communal worship. What is more, their uncleanness was transferable to others—anything or anyone they touched would become temporarily unclean. Jesus not only healed lepers, he actually reached out and touched them (Matt 8:3 and parallel passages). His healing ministry not only served as a sign of the coming Kingdom of God, but also of his compassion for those marginalized by society.

JESUS' TRIAL AND DEATH

The Gospels do not hesitate to identify Jesus' enemies. They include not only religious figures, but political figures, as well. Luke tells us that Herod Antipas, who was responsible for the execution of John the Baptist, also sought to kill Jesus (Luke 13:32), but it does not say why. Perhaps he felt Jesus was a threat because of his popularity with the masses—or perhaps Jesus' teaching on divorce hit too close to home, given Herod Antipas's personal life. In any event, Antipas was not responsible for Jesus' arrest, which occurred in Jerusalem, not in Antipas's realm of Galilee. Rather, the procedure was initiated by the Jerusalem Sanhedrin. The fear expressed by the Sanhedrin that Jesus would draw all the people to him and incite the Romans to destroy the nation (John 11:47–48) was real. The elephant in the living room that no one mentioned was the Jewish resistance movement. Since the death of Herod the Great, the nation had erupted in rebellion on several occasions. All the people needed, it seemed, was a charismatic leader to unite them in a cause, and they would willingly rise up against their overlords.

Jesus' trial before the Sanhedrin did not follow some of the procedures outlined in later rabbinic literature. For instance, while rabbinic tradition prescribed that the defense was to be presented first, the Gospels record that Jesus' accusers spoke first, and that no defense was actually given. Also, rabbinic law prohibited the Sanhedrin from convening at night, or on a feast day. Jesus' trial was conducted in the night after Jesus had celebrated the Passover. Furthermore, a guilty verdict was supposed to be announced on the day after the trial, but Jesus was proclaimed guilty immediately. And the list goes on.[1] Some Christians have

---

1. For a typical treatment, see Earle L. Wingo, *The Illegal Trial of Jesus* (Ontario, CA: Chick, 2009).

pointed out these discrepancies as further evidence of the injustice of Jesus' death, but skeptics have instead used them to argue that the entire trial of Jesus as recorded in the Gospels is a fraud. In fact, neither opinion is justified: we cannot say for certain when the procedures described by the rabbis were established. Indeed, the accounts of Josephus and the New Testament seem to indicate that the rabbinic descriptions of the legal system of Judea were more idealizations than reality.

Why was Jesus sent to Pontius Pilate after the Sanhedrin trial? The Sanhedrin had determined that Jesus' crime was worthy of death, and the Jews had been deprived of the right to carry out this penalty when Judea was placed under the procurators (see John 18:31; Josephus, *War* 2:117). While there were clearly cases of mob violence where the Jews took it upon themselves to execute insignificant troublemakers like the deacon Stephen (Acts 6–7), they could not take action in so high a profile case as that of Jesus. It was essential that everyone follow proper protocol. According to Luke (Luke 23:6–12), Pontius Pilate had sent Jesus to Antipas when he learned that Jesus was a Galilean. Apparently it was considered a courtesy to send a prisoner back to the country of their origin for trial, though it was not required by Roman law. Antipas questioned Jesus and mocked him, but returned him to Pilate, since Jesus was being charged with inciting trouble in Jerusalem.

One of the most controversial aspects of the Gospel accounts of Jesus' trial has been the reluctance of Pontius Pilate to render a decision regarding Jesus. Many writers have argued that the scenario seems implausible, given what is known of Pilate's cruelty. Some even argue that Pilate is depicted as reluctant in order to exonerate the Romans from guilt in the crucifixion, and to fix the blame solely on the back of the Jewish officials. While we should not feel compelled to defend the historicity of all the details of the Gospel accounts, given that these texts contain some theologizing and reconstruction, the picture of Pilate presented in the Gospels does not seem so improbable. Since Pilate was already in a precarious position with Rome because of his mismanagement of Jewish affairs, he would probably have been reluctant to become involved in controversy over a Galilean prophet.[2] Furthermore, Pilate may have believed that executing a Galilean with dubious cause could result in Herod Antipas lodging a complaint. Pilate had previously executed some Galilean Jews within his realm (Luke 13:1), and that incident may well

---

2. See Philo, *Legatio* 299–305.

been the cause of friction between him and Herod Antipas mentioned in Luke 23:12. Given his delicate political situation, it would have been better to avoid controversy. And finally, Pilate could surely be cruel, but he was not given to executing people without provocation. Even in the case that led to his recall—attacking the Samaritans who were heading to Mt. Gerizim to see the appearance of the Temple vessels—Pilate was not acting out of total capriciousness or cruelty. Even Josephus observed that the pilgrims were armed.[3]

The Gospel accounts of Jesus' trial before Pilate ring with authentic details. The fact that there was a Roman trial is evident from the fact that Jesus was crucified in Roman fashion, rather than stoned to death, in Jewish style. He was not charged with blasphemy, which would have been of no interest to Rome, but with sedition—of claiming to be the "king of the Jews," and thus challenging the absolute authority of Caesar. Such a crime would indeed have brought the dreaded penalty of crucifixion. After acceding to the demands of the crowd and condemning Jesus to death, Pilate washed his hands. In this case, the procedure was not designed to remove guilt, but as a public demonstration of innocence. The treatment Jesus received before his crucifixion was typical of that doled out upon the victims of Roman justice. The condemned prisoner received a flogging with the *flagellum*, the corded whip that literally shredded the skin of the prisoner. Also typical was the mockery he received from the Roman guards. Crucifixion was a public demonstration of the folly of defying the power of Rome. It was designed to put the victims on display and humiliate them even more than it was to torture them. There was no standard method for crucifixion, however, so we cannot actually know the exact shape of Jesus' cross or the details of the procedure. Nonetheless, several New Testament texts state that Jesus was nailed to his cross (John 20:25; Acts 2:23; Col 2:14), and not simply tied, as was sometimes done.

The *titulus* placed over Jesus' head stated the crime for which he had been condemned: "Jesus of Nazareth, King of the Jews." There can be little doubt that Pilate had not meant this plaque to be a declaration of his faith in Jesus. Instead, it was meant as an insult to the Jews. Pilate was demonstrating that even the greatest of the Jews, their king, could not escape the power of Roman justice.

3. See *Ant.* 18:86.

THE BURIAL OF JESUS

The mode of Jesus' burial has long been a subject of debate among scholars. It is of crucial importance, since it impinges heavily on the question of his resurrection. For instance, if Jesus were not really buried, but his body merely left on the cross or tossed on the trash heap (as often was done with victims of crucifixion), then the accounts of the resurrection are obvious fictions. Or if, as some have argued, his body were only temporarily placed in Joseph of Arimathea's tomb to be moved after the Sabbath day, the tomb would have indeed been empty on Easter morning, but only because the corpse was elsewhere. Our understanding of the cultural practices of the first century can thus deeply influence the way we conceive the central event of the Christian faith, the resurrection of Jesus.

While it was typical for the Romans to leave the bodies of the crucified on the cross, it was not unusual for the corpses to be given to family members or others who might request them. A rich member of the Jewish Sanhedrin would surely have the clout to make such a request. But the burial of someone who had been crucified might have been a complicated affair. Rabbinic tradition said that such accursed bodies were to be buried far away from the city. But the accuracy of this tradition is debatable on a couple bases: first, because rabbinic tradition often represents ideal, rather than actual cases; and second, because the bones of a crucified man were actually found in an ossuary in Israel in 1968 (see Chapter 5). While the burial of a crucified man like Jesus might have been unusual, there is no reason to regard it as unlikely.

According to very ancient tradition, the burial place of Jesus was located at a site now marked by the Church of the Holy Sepulcher, in the city of Jerusalem. The presence of some first-century tombs on the site demonstrate that the area was, in fact, used as a burial place in the time of Jesus. But the cave that might have served as Jesus' resting place no longer exists. It was damaged around AD 140 when the Roman Emperor Hadrian erected a pagan temple on the site. Then, in AD 1009, the Muslim ruler Al Hakim had the cave carved away, so nothing of the original tomb remains. Some scholars, however, have favored the identification of another tomb as Jesus' burial place: the so-called Garden Tomb, located just outside of Jerusalem. Unlike the tombs in the Church of the Holy Sepulcher, this tomb was sealed in antiquity with a huge carved stone, shaped like a large millstone, which was rolled into a special slot in front of the entrance. It was relatively easy to roll into place, but it would have taken several strong men to dislodge it (or one mighty angel).

CONCLUSION

The world in which Jesus lived was in many ways very different from our own. The beliefs and attitudes of the average person were shaped by events and ideas far removed from the daily experience of the modern Westerner. Fortunately, ancient texts and artifacts have helped us to reconstruct much of that worldview. Perhaps we cannot put ourselves in the shoes of an ancient Palestinian Jew, but we can know what those shoes looked like, maybe how they were made, and how they might have fit.

But when we turn our attention to Jesus, we recognize that history and culture cannot tell us all there is to be said about this man. Jesus was a person of his time and culture, but he was much more than that. The teachings of Jesus cannot be comprehended merely by comparing and contrasting them with the doctrines and dogmas of his day. Jesus' significance cannot be explained simply in terms of his impact on a particular land and people. Like all great individuals, Jesus transcended his time and his society. But Jesus did more than just transcend his time. Rather, we might say that he confined himself to his time, but only partially so. Because for people of every land and time who have placed their faith in him, he has become part of their age, living in them and through them, forever.

Bibliography

THIS BIBLIOGRAPHY IS INTENDED to guide the reader in further reading and research on various topics presented in the chapters and to provide full references for the books and articles cited in the footnotes. Hopefully it will prove helpful to readers wishing to delve deeper into Jesus' historical and cultural background.

Achtemeir, Paul J., et. al. *Introducing the New Testament: Its Literature and Theology.* Grand Rapids, MI: Eerdmans, 2001.
Adler, Jerry and Anne Underwood. "Search for the Sacred," *Newsweek*, August 30, 2004.
Arnold, Clinton, ed. *Zondervan Illustrated Bible Backgrounds Commentary: New Testament.* Grand Rapids: Zondervan, 2002.
Associated Press. "Archaeologists Find Tomb of King Herod." *The New York Times*, May 9, 2007.
Bauckham, Richard. *Jesus and the Eyewitnesses: The Gospels as Eyewitness Testimony.* Grand Rapids, MI: Eerdmans, 2006.
Blenkinsopp, Joseph, et. al. *Families in Ancient Israel.* Louisville: Westminster John Knox, 1997.
Blomberg, Craig. *The Historical Reliability of the Gospels.* Downers Grove, IL: Intervarsity, 2008.
Brenton, Lancelot. *The Septuagint with Apocrypha.* Peabody, MA: Hendrickson, 1986.
Bright, John. *A History of Israel*, fourth ed. Philadelphia: Westminster/John Knox, 1999.
Brisco, Thomas C. *Holman Bible Atlas: A Complete Guide to the Expansive Geography of Biblical History.* Broadman & Holman Reference. Nashville: B&H Publishing Group, 1999.
Bruce Chilton, *Rabbi Jesus: An Intimate Biography.* New York: Image/Doubleday, 2000.
Bruce, F. F. *New Testament History.* Garden City, NY: Doubleday/Galilee, 1983.
Bruce, F. F. *The New Testament Documents: Are They Reliable?* Reprint. Grand Rapids, MI: Eerdmans, 2003.
Carter, Warren. *The Roman Empire and the New Testament: An Essential Guide.* Nashville: Abingdon, 2006.
Chancey, Mark A. *The Myth of a Gentile Galilee.* Cambridge: Cambridge University Press, 2002.
Charles, R. H. *Apocrypha and Pseudepigrapha of the Old Testament*, 2 volumes. Oxford: Clarendon Press, 1913.
Charlesworth, James (ed.), *The Old Testament Pseudepigrapha*, 2 volumes. Garden City, N.Y.: Doubleday, 1985.

Clint E. Arnold, ed. *The Zondervan Illustrated Bible Backgrounds Commentary, Volume 1: Matthew, Mark, Luke*. Grand Rapids: Zondervan, 2002.

Collins, John J. *The Scepter and the Star: The Messiahs of the Dead Sea Scrolls and Other Ancient Literature*. New York: Doubleday, 1995.

Currid, John. *Doing Archaeology in the Land of the Bible: A Basic Guide*. Grand Rapids: Baker, 1999.

Danby, Herbert. *The Mishnah*. Oxford: Oxford University Press, 1933.

DeSilva, David. *Honor, Patronage, Kinship & Purity: Unlocking New Testament Culture*. Downers Grove, IL: Intervarsity, 2000.

Eddy, Paul and Gregory Boyd. *The Jesus Legend: A Case for the Historical Reliability of the Synoptic Jesus Tradition*. Grand Rapids, MI: Baker, 2007.

Evans, Craig A. *Jesus and the Ossuaries: What Jewish Burial Practices Reveal about the Beginning of Christianity*. Waco: Baylor University Press, 2003.

Evans, Craig, ed. *A Dictionary of New Testament Background*. Downers Grove, IL: Intervarsity, 2000.

Evans, Craig. *Fabricating Jesus: How Modern Scholars Distort the Gospels*. Downers Grove, IL: InterVarsity, 2006.

Ferguson, Everett. *Backgrounds of Early Christianity*, 3rd ed. Grand Rapids, MI: Eerdmans, 2003.

Frankfort, Henri, et. al. *The Intellectual Adventure of Ancient Man: An Essay on Speculative Thought in the Ancient Near East*. Reprint. Chicago: University of Chicago Press, 1977.

Gower, Ralph. *New Manners and Customs of Bible Times*. Chicago: Moody, 1987.

Grant, Michael. *The Jews in the Roman World*. New York: Charles Scribner's Sons, 1973.

Hengel, Martin. *Crucifixion*. Philadelphia: Fortress, 1977.

Hengel, Martin. *Judaism and Hellenism*. Philadelphia: Fortress, 1974.

Horsley, Richard, and John Hanson. *Bandits, Prophets, and Messiahs: Popular Movements at the Time of Jesus*. San Francisco: Harper and Row, 1985.

Jacobovici, Simcha and Charles Pellegrino, *The Jesus Family Tomb: The Discovery, the Investigation, and the Evidence That Could Change History*. San Francisco: HarperCollins, 2007.

Jill-Levine, Amy. *The Misunderstood Jew: The Church and the Scandal of the Jewish Jesus*. San Francisco: Harper, 2007.

McRay, John. *Archeology and the New Testament*. Grand Rapids, MI: Baker, 1991.

Merrill, Eugene. *Kingdom of Priests: A History of Old Testament Israel*. Grand Rapids: Baker, 1996.

Miller, James Maxwell and John Haralson Hayes, *A History of Ancient Israel and Judah*. Louisville: Westminster/John Knox Press, 2006.

Neusner, Jacob, et. al., eds. *Judaisms and their Messiahs at the Turn of the Christian Era*. Cambridge: Cambridge University Press, 1988.

Page, Charles. *The Land and the Book: An Introduction to the World of the Bible*. Nashville: Abingdon, 1993.

Raymond Brown, *An Introduction to New Testament Christology*. Mahwah, NJ: Paulist, 1994.

Richardson, Peter. *Herod: King of the Jews and Friend of the Romans*. Columbia, SC: University of South Carolina Press, 1996.

Roetzel, Calvin. *The World that Shaped the New Testament*. Westminster/John Knox, 2002.

Rousseau, John J. K. and Rami Arav. *Jesus and His World: An Archaeological and Cultural Dictionary*. Minneapolis: Fortress, 1995.

Safrai, S. and M. Stern. *The Jewish People in the First Century: Compendia Rerum Iudaicarum et Novum Testamentum*. Assen: van Gorcum and Philadelphia: Fortress, 1987.

Sanders, E. P. *Judaism: Practice & Belief: 63 BCE -66 CE*. Philadelphia: Trinity Press International, 1991.

Schiffman, Lawrence H. *Texts and Traditions: A Source Reader for the Study of Second Temple and Rabbinic Judaism*. Hoboken, NJ: Ktav, 1998.

Schürer, Emile. *A History of the Jewish People in the Age of Jesus Christ*, ed. Geza Vermes, Fergus Millar, and Matthew Black. 4 vols. Edinburgh: T. & T. Clark, 1973-1987.

Scott, J. Julius Jr. *Jewish Backgrounds of the New Testament*. Grand Rapids, MI: Baker, 2000.

Smallwood, E. Mary. *The Jews Under Roman Rule: From Pompey to Diocletian*. Leiden: Brill, 2001.

Tomasino, Anthony. *Judaism Before Jesus: The Events and Ideas that Shaped the New Testament World*. Downers Grove, IL: Intervarsity, 2003.

Tzaferis, Vassilios. "Crucifixion—The Archaeological Evidence." *Biblical Archaeology Review* 11, February 1985.

VanderKam, James. *An Introduction to Early Judaism*. Grand Rapids, MI: Eerdmans, 2001.

Vermes, Geza. *Jesus in his Jewish Context*. Philadelphia: Augsburg Fortress, 2003.

Vermes, Geza. *The Complete Dead Sea Scrolls in English*. New York/London: Penguin, 1997.

Walton, J. H. "Exodus, Date of," in *Dictionary of the Old Testament: Pentateuch*, ed. T. D. Alexander and D. W. Baker, 258-272. Downers' Grove, IL: InterVarsity Press, 2003.

Wingo, Earle L. *The Illegal Trial of Jesus*. Ontario, CA: Chick, 2009.

Wright, N. T. *Jesus and the Victory of God*. Philadelphia: Augsburg Fortress, 1997.

Wright, N. T. *Who Was Jesus?* Grand Rapids, MI: Eerdmans, 1993.

Wright, R. B. "Psalms of Solomon." In *Old Testament Pseudepigrapha*, vol. 2, edited by James H. Charlesworth. Garden City, NY: Doubleday, 1985.

Scripture Index

OLD TESTAMENT

Genesis

5:13	35
5:18–23	16
6:1	4
9:20–27	86
17	114
34:12	101

Exodus

1:11	36
2:1	78
3:6	128
6:15–25	36
12:37	36
12:40	35
13:12–13	117
18:17–26	75
28:1–2	118

Leviticus

8:10–12	132
12	96
16	118
19:32	86
20:18	78
21:16–23	118
24:19–20	79

Numbers

11:16–17	75
12:1–15	144
18:15	117
24–30	75

Deuteronomy

6:4	112, 122
19:15	76
21:18–21	85
21:22	80
24:1	102
25:3	78

Judges

8:14	77
11:5	77

Ruth

4:2	77

1 Samuel

4	119
10:1	132
18:20–25	101

2 Samuel

7	36, 132
7:14	4
7:16	133

1 Kings

2:35	119
11:3	94
16:24–25	29
21:8	77

2 Kings

15:5	144

2 Chronicles

16:14	105
26:16–20	144

Ezra

4:1–5	111
5:5	75
7:6	113, 123
7:11–26	113
8:2	120

Nehemiah

4	111

Job

13:4	104
42:13–15	94

Psalms

16	128
49	128
90:10	104
105:15	132
107:32	75

Proverbs

4:1–9	97
31	91

Isaiah

9:1–7	133
11:1–10	133
28:13	97
61:1–2	5, 143

Jeremiah

8:22–9:6	104
23:5–6	133
30:39	133

Ezekiel

8:11	75
34:23–24	133
37	128
37:24–25	133

Daniel

7	134, 140
12	128
12:1	134

Hosea

11:1	4

Micah

5:1–5	133
5:2	2

Zechariah

3:1–7	134

Malachi

2:7	118

# Scripture Index

NEW TESTAMENT

Matthew

Reference	Page
1:19–25	2
2:1–15	2
2:16–18	57
3:13–17	2
4:1–11	2
4:3	4
4:12–17	3
5:14	142
5:17–48	3
5:27–30	3
5:31–32	3
5:38–42	3
5:38–47	131–132, 141
7:29	123
8:3	144
9:12	104, 143
9:18–22	143
12:5	139
13:31–35	3
13:53–57	139
13:55	138
14	65
14:1–12	66
14:14	5
15:1–20	3
15:14	23
15:21–28	139
15:24	107
16:21	6
17:15	103
19:3–9	141
19:3–12	66
20:28	6
21:33–41	6
22:23–32	128
23	126
23:15	126
23:23	126
24:30	3
25:1–13	142
25:64–66	7
26:62–66	75
27:57	75

Mark

Reference	Page
1:9–11	2
1:12–13	2
1:14–15	3
2:5	143
2:10–12	3
2:23–28	126
3:1–5	3
3:1–6	6
6	65
6:2–4	139
6:3	100
6:14–29	66
7:2–4	124
9:17–18	103
10:32–34	6
10:45	6
11:12–18	6
12:1–12	6
12:28–34	118
14:53–63	75
14:61	4

Luke

Reference	Page
1	2
1:1–4	26
1:8–9	119
1:32	4
2:1–3	2
2:2–5	137
2:41–51	138
2:41–52	2
3:21–22	2
3:23	2
4:1–13	2

Luke - continued

4:17–20	5
6:26–29	3
7:22	5
7:22–23	143
9:7–9	66
9:39	103
12:13–21	72
13:1	145
13:31–35	6
13:32	65, 144
15:11–32	142
16:18	3
16:19–31	72
19:12	142
19:12–26	64
23:6–12	145
23:12	146
23:50	75

John

1:29–36	2
2:12–17	6
3:1	75
3:16	4
4	141
4:9	111
4:20	115
4:22	139
5:2	25
5:14	143
5:25	4
6:35	4
9:1–3	143
10:14–18	6
10:30	4
10:36	4
11	5
11:25	4–5
11:47–48	144
11:49–50	6
12:37	5
13:31–32	81
14:6	4
14:9	4
18:31	77, 145
18:36	3, 141
19:13	25
19:38–39	75
20:25	146
21:25	26

Acts

1:3	7
1:11	7
2:23	146
4:1–4	127, 129
5:17–18	127, 129
5:35–39	135
6–7	145
12	60
13:16	111
17:29–32	125
19:11–17	142
23:1–5	75
23:6–8	75
23:8	125
23:9	126, 129
25–26	66

Romans

1:7	24

1 Corinthians

1:17	24
7:10	24
9:14	24
11:23	24
11:23–25	24
11:26–26	24
15:4	24
15:6–7	24

2 Corinthians

11:24	79

Galatians

2:9	24
3:13	24
4:4	24

Philippians

2:8	24
2:9	24

Colossians

2:14	146

1 Thessalonians

2:14–16	24
4:13–17	24

Jude

14	16

Subject Index

A

Agrapha, 22–23
Agrippa I, 66-67
Alexander Janneus, 19, 48, 77, 80
Alexander the Great, 97, 111, 136
    conquests of, 33, 40, 87, 111
    tutor of, 91
    worship of, 109
Alexandria, 19, 104, 130
    citizens of, 53
    city of, 41, 43, 53, 55, 91–92
    synagogue in, 41
Angels, 4, 15, 95, 104, 125, 129
    and Jesus, 4, 7, 148
    and Jewish sects, 125–126, 129
    and Old Testament, 15, 134
    and Persians, 95
Antigonus, 47, 52, 55–57, 61
Antiochus III, 42
Antiochus IV Epiphanes, 15, 42–44
Antiochus VII, 46
Antipater (father of Herod the Great), 49, 52–55
Antipater (son of Herod the Great), 62–63
Antony, 55–56, 58–59, 70, 72–73
    and Cleopatra, 55, 58–59, 70, 72
    and Herod, 56, 58–59
    and Octavian, 55, 59, 70, 72
Apion, 20, 88, 113,
Apocrypha, 17, 81, 92, 103
    as canon, 14–15
    contents of, 15, 81, 103
    origins of, 14
Aramaic, 6, 18, 44, 74, 84, 95, 122, 131, 134
    and Apocrypha, 14–16
    and Jesus, 89
    and Babylonian Exile, 88–89, 95
    in Roman texts, 84
    in Syria, 33
Archelaus, 64, 67, 73, 142
Archeology, 10–12, 25
Aristobulus I, 47
Aristobulus II, 52
Aristobulus III, 58
Aristotle, 91
Astrology, 22, 137
Augustus (Octavian), 55, 64, 67, 70–73, 86, 136–137
    and Herod, 60,
    and royal cult, 110
    declared emperor, 70
    defeats Mark Antony, 59
    successor of, 65

B

Babylonian Exile, 89, 117
    and messianism, 133
    and synagogues, 120
    beginning of, 37
Ben Sira, 15, 17, 123

C

Circumcision
    and Gentiles, 112, 114
    in other nations, 92
    outlawing of, 43
    ritual of, 96–97
Cleopatra
    Cleopatra III, 48
    Cleopatra VII, 31, 53, 55, 58–59, 70, 72–73

Crucifixion, 80
    practice of, 80–82
    of Jesus, 7, 13, 107, 145–147
Cyrus the Great, 39, 138
    frees captives, 37

D

Daniel, Book of
    and Jesus, 140
    and messianism, 134
    and resurrection, 128
Dead Sea Scrolls, 11, 16–17, 66, 92, 135
    and messianism, 133–134
    and practice, 118, 137
    and scripture, 113
    community of, 131
Decapolis, 33
Diaspora, 14, 32, 120
    and language, 88
Diet, 61, 84, 99, 103
Divorce
    during New Testament times, 101–102
    Jesus' teaching, 3, 66, 141
    of Alexander's officers, 87
    of Herod Antipas, 65, 144
    of Herod the Great, 62

E

Enoch, 16–17
Essenes, 104, 124, 130
    Dead Sea Scroll sect, 17
    on marriage, 100
    practices of, 130–131
Exorcism
    Jesus' practice, 5, 26, 142–143

F

Fasting
    of Jesus, 2, 140
Flagellum, 79–80, 146

Free will
    and the Jewish sects, 129–130
Fourth Philosophy, 131–132

G

Galilee, 13, 20, 27, 48, 71, 97
    Antipas tetrarch of, 64–66, 144
    geography of, 29–33
    Herod governor of, 54, 77
    inhabitants of, 83, 89, 99, 107
    Jesus in, 2–3, 11–12, 139, 140
Gerizim, 68
    temple on, 33, 47, 110–111, 141, 146
Gilead, 29
Gospels, 2–5, 17, 22–26, 84, 89, 103, 124, 126–127, 138–139, 141, 143–145
Greek language, 40
    Jesus' knowledge of, 88–89

H

Hasmoneans, 48, 51, 58, 63, 116
    and the high priesthood, 44–46, 50, 56, 119, 129, 134
    and resistance, 44
Hellenism, 40–41, 79, 87–88, 90, 94–95
Herod Antipas (son of Herod the Great), 65–67, 73, 144–146
Herod the Great, 142, 144
    and the temple, 116
    and Jesus, 1, 57, 136
    Kingship, 67, 73, 77, 110, 119
High priest, 37–38, 58, 61, 67, 98, 118–119, 134–135
    and Jesus, 4, 6–7
    and Sadducees, 129
    and Sanhedrin, 75–78
    and Temple, 61, 64
    as rulers, 41–56
Hillel, 76, 102, 141
Hyrcanus II, 48, 50, 77

I

Idumeans, 31, 47, 92
Infanticide, 57, 63, 94, 96, 138

J

Jamnia, 113
Jason, 42–43
Jerusalem, 133, 144, 147
  and Hasmoneans, 44–49
  and Herod the Great, 54–62, 116
  and the Romans, 50–59, 64, 78, 95, 123, 134, 141
  archeology in, 11–12
  burials in, 11, 80, 147
  geography of, 25, 28–33
  governors of, 68, 95, 145
  officials in, 6
  religious establishment in, 17, 107
  Sanhedrin in, 75–77, 144
  sieges of, 37, 134
  Temple in, 36, 37, 44, 61, 64, 77, 107, 110–111, 114–120, 134–135, 139, 141
  under Seleucids, 42–44
  Upper City, 11
John, Gospel of
  and archeology, 25
  as historical, 25–26
  compared to synoptic gospels, 24
  on Jesus, 141
  on political establishment, 127
  origins, 25–26
  sayings in, 26
  written to, 26
John Hyrcanus
  as high priest, 46
  death of, 47
  destroying Samaria, 60, 111
John the Baptist, 130
  and Jesus, 2–3, 5, 139, 143–144
  execution of, 65–66, 144
Josephus, 31–32, 38, 74, 88, 102, 138, 141, 145–146
  History of, 19–22
  on Antigonus I, 56
  on Archelaus, 67
  on canon, 113
  on the Essenes, 104, 130–131
  on Fourth Philosophy, 131
  on Herod the Great, 57, 63–64
  on the High Priest, 75–76
  on Hyrcanus, 47
  on Jesus, 76, 137
  on John the Baptist, 66
  on Messiah, 134
  on Pilate, 68
  on Pharisees, 123–126
  on Sadducees, 127–129
  reliability of, 22
  religion of, 21
Judas Maccabeus, 44–45
Julius Caesar, 86, 136
  and Herod the Great, 110
  and the Jews, 52
  assassination, 54–55, 70

K

Kingdom of God
  according to Jesus, 3, 131–132
  Jewish expectations of, 140
  that is coming, 134, 143–144

L

Law, oral, 18, 66
  and Pharisees, 124, 126

M

Marriage
  and family, 86–87, 93, 95
  Antipas, 65
  customs of, 100–102
  Essenes' practice, 130
  intermarriage, 113
  of David, 57
Mattathias
  Hezekiah Ben Mattathias, 81
  Mattathias Hashmon, 44, 56

Messiah
    and Dead Sea Scrolls, 133
    Davidic Messiah, 134-135
    Jesus as, 2, 4-5, 7, 126, 129, 132, 143
    Jewish expectations, 5, 129, 132, 134
    meaning, 4, 132
    priestly Messiah, 134
Mishnah, 18-19, 79
    on marriage, 100, 102, 105
    on Sanhedrin, 76-77
Monotheism, 112

N

Nabatea, 50, 64, 65
    and Herod, 56, 58-59
    and Janeus, 48
    Aretas III, 49

O

Octavian (see Augustus)
Origen, 14, 19
Ossuary, 11, 81, 106, 147

P

Palestine, 99
    and Apocrypha, 14
    and Jesus, 27, 136
    and the Romans, 13, 71, 95
    archeology of, 11
    climate of, 30-31
    geography of, 28-30
    Jewish religious beliefs in, 107, 120, 126
    people of, 31-34, 36-37, 62, 88-89, 107-108, 120-121, 126
    region of, 27-28
    rulers of, 40-42, 54-55, 108
Parables, 3, 6, 18, 141-142
Pentateuch
    and the Sadducees, 114, 128-129
    Samaritan Pentateuch, 111, 114
Pharisees, 72, 75
    against Janneus, 48
    and Christians, 125-126
    and Essenes, 130-131
    and the Fourth Philosophy, 131
    and Hyrcanus, 49
    and Sadducees, 125, 127-130, 135, 141
    as enemies of Jesus, 5, 126, 139
    as religious leaders, 5, 124, 126
    beliefs of, 5-6, 18, 123-125, 127-128, 130
    origins of, 124
Philip (son of Herod the Great), 63-67
Philo of Alexandria, 104
    as historian, 19, 130-131
    as philosopher, 19, 91
    history of, 19, 88
Philosophy
    Epicureans, 91, 124
    in Palestine, 92
    of Philo, 19, 91
    of Plato, 91, 109, 124
    Stoics, 124
    the Fourth Philosophy, 131-132
Phoenicia, 28, 32-33, 84, 91-92
Plato, 91
Polis, 42
Pompey, 49-52
Pontius Pilate
    and Jesus, 7, 13, 21, 145-146
    as Governor, 68, 74, 77, 95
Pseudepigrapha, 16-17, 23, 92
Ptolemy I Soter, 41
Ptolemy Lathyrus, 48
Ptolemy XIII, 53

Q

Qumran, 11, 17, 134, 140

R

Rabbinic Literature, 92, 113, 123-130, 144
Rome, 55, 64
    and Christians, 13

Rome - continued
    and the Greeks, 42–43, 90
    and Herod, 57–62
    and Jesus, 7, 129, 140
    and Jews, 1, 13, 20, 140, 145
    and Palestine, 49–53, 56–57, 59–68, 78, 142
    and the senate, 69–74
    as City, 13, 26, 34, 70, 104
    emperors of, 13, 20, 53, 69–74, 107
    practices of, 6, 50, 70–74, 78, 90, 107, 110
    wars of, 13, 69–74, 90

S

Sabbath
    and Jesus, 3, 5, 7, 126, 141, 147
    and Rabbinic Judaism, 18, 105
    and Samaritans, 112
    Jewish practice of, 18, 43–44, 77, 96, 105, 114, 120, 125–126
Salome
    Salome Alexandra, 48–49, 75, 77
    sister of Herod, 59, 62
    Herod's step daughter, 66
Samaritans
    and the Jews, 32–33, 67, 73, 110–111, 115, 141
    and Rome, 68
    history of, 32–33, 37, 110
    religious practices of, 47, 110–111, 114–115, 128, 141
Sanhedrin, 52, 67, 125
    and Herod, 54, 61
    and Janneus, 77
    and Jesus, 78, 144–145, 147
    details of, 74–78, 144
Scribe
    Christian scribes, 21, 23, 100
    Jewish scribes, 15, 118, 122–123
Seleucus I, 40
Sepphoris, 64–65, 89, 139, 142
Simon Hasmoneus, 46
Son of God, 4

Son of man
    as Jesus, 4
    in Daniel, 134
Suetonius, 12–13
Synagogue, 41
    and Gentiles, 112, 139
    and Jesus, 2, 121
    institution of, 120–122

T

Tacitus, 13
Talmud, 18–19, 31, 97
    and Sanhedrin, 75
    compilation of, 98
    teachings of, 78 102
Teacher of Righteousness, 135
Temple, 52, 75–78, 96, 120, 122, 134–135
    abuse of, 6, 43–44, 50, 64, 68, 79, 95
    and community at Qumran, 17
    and gentiles, 79, 139
    and Jesus, 6, 17, 138, 141
    and Sadducees, 127, 129
    destruction of, 37, 115, 131, 141
    Herod's Temple, 61–62, 90, 115
    in Samaria, 47, 60, 110–111, 146
    layout of, 116–117
    of Solomon, 28, 36–37, 120, 132
    pagan temples, 60, 107–108, 147
    Second Temple, 43–45, 49, 111, 116, 122
    worship in, 110, 114–119

V

Vespasian, 20

Z

Zealots. See Fourth Philosophy
Zeus, 44, 108